The Plumb Club Symposium

Saturday, May 31st, 2014
Mandalay Bay, Las Vegas, NV

"Branding Your Store While Swimming with Sharks"

Featuring an exclusive presentation by
"Shark Tank" personality

Daymond John

The Daymond John "brand" is all about being out in front and going your own way. In *The Brand Within*, he gets readers thinking about what it means to succeed in business and in life. One thing about Daymond, he takes charge, and here he puts his own spin on our consumer culture and challenges us to change things up.

—*Mark Burnett, Famed Television Producer*

What a treat it is to sit beside Daymond John on *The Shark Tank*! He's full of surprises, but it's no surprise that he's just as smart and funny and cutting-edge in print as he is on the set. This is a book for anyone who wants to rock their own worlds, the same way Daymond keeps rocking' his, and ours.

—*Barbara Corcoran, Real estate Mogul and Business Consultant*

The Brand Within is the ultimate hustler's handbook, whether you're selling records, clothes, cars or your own image! Daymond drops jewels in a simplistic way so that anybody can understand the world of Branding. *The Brand Within* is good money.

—*Fabolous, Hip-hop Recording Star*

AMAZING! *The Brand Within* is a great read! As I build the Kim Kardashian Brand, I understand the importance of aligning myself with those who reflect the same elegance, beauty, fashion, and excellence as I do. Daymond helps you to realize the importance of perception and how it is conveyed to the world. Building your brand never stops and after reading this book, you'll be inspired to keep thriving.

—*Kim Kardashian, Model, Actress and Businesswoman*

WOW! After finishing *The Brand Within*, I realized even more the importance of my personal brand and how others may perceive me, when I'm not even thinking about it! The Shark lays down in detail the ways to improve your public image. This in return will improve your chances of success—true knowledge for any and all who want to make it in the game of life on their own terms.

—*Terrence J, Co- host of BET's 106 and Park*

A must read for anyone who wants their brand to walk into the room long before they do.

—*Kevin O'Leary, Renowned Entrepreneur and Venture Capitalist*

THE
BRAND
WITHIN

The Power of Branding
From Birth to the Boardroom

Daymond John

with

Daniel Paisner

Published originally in 2010 by Display of Power Publishing, Inc., New York, New York.
www.displayofpower.com / www.daymondjohn.com

This edition published May 2014 by Dunham Books, Franklin, Tennessee. All rights re-
served. No part of this book may be reproduced in any form or by any means, electronic,
mechanical, photocopying, scanning, or otherwise, without permission in writing from the
publisher, except by a reviewer who may quote brief passages in a review. For information on
licensing, permissions or special sales, contact the publisher at info@dunhamgroupinc.com

ISBN# 978-1-939447-54-8 (Trade paperback)
     # 978-1-939447-55-5 (ebook)

Printed in the United States of America

Cover design by: wes@confid3ntial.com
Interior design and layout by Darlene Swanson • www.van-garde.com

A special dedication to:

MY MOTHER: You are one of those very few people who has the gift of making people strive to become the best personal brand they can be. You have clearly done this for me. You instill confidence, hope, and power in everybody fortunate enough to know you and ask for nothing in return! It's a true honor to be your son. With all my heart, thank you!

MY EX-WIFE: As parents, it is very difficult to raise children if both parents don't have the same morals, goals, and visions in mind. I'm proud to say that your undying dedication and standards are something I will never have to question. Thank you!

MY GIRLS: It's very easy to preach and tell other people what they should do and shouldn't do, but the true evidence of whether a person truly does live by the standards he preaches is to see how his children develop into adults. When I see how you both work hard for what you want and don't expect anybody to give it to you, it makes me strive even harder to push myself to the limit! You girls are a pure reflection of the brand that your parents have worked so hard to maintain. You show the kind of discipline, hard work, and drive that will be needed to make you the brand that people from near and far will search out to be associated with. I'm very proud to say that I am your dad. Thank you!

I would like to thank all of the people, personal and professional, who have believed in the Daymond John brand. I've been honestly blessed with many good people in my life, from partners to friends to family to even enemies, who have made me a better person. I will continue to strive to become a better person who makes this world a better place. As the legendary radio DJ Frankie "Hollywood" Crocker used to say, "I hope you live to be one hundred years old, and me, one hundred years but minus a day, so that I will never know that good people like you passed away."

Contents

Brand

Main Entry:
   ¹brand
Pronunciation:
   \'brand\
Function:
   noun
Etymology:
   Middle English, torch, sword, from Old English; akin to Old English *bærnan* to burn
Date:
   before 12th century

1(a) a charred piece of wood (b) firebrand 1(c) something (as lightning) that resembles a firebrand 2: sword 3a (1) a mark made by burning with a hot iron to attest manufacture or quality or to designate ownership (2) a printed mark made for similar purposes : trademark, b (1) a mark put on criminals with a hot iron (2) a mark of disgrace : stigma <the *brand* of poverty> 4(a) a class of goods identified by name as the product of a single firm or manufacturer : make (b) a characteristic or distinctive kind <a lively *brand* of theater> (c) brand name : a tool used to produce a brand

Main Entry:
   ²brand
Function:
   transitive verb
Date:
   15th century

1: to mark with a brand 2: to mark with disapproval : stigmatize <he was *branded* a coward> 3: to impress indelibly <*brand* the lesson on his mind>

■ Merriam-Webster's Online Dictionary ■

Brand

Main Entry:
> ¹brand

Pronunciation:
> \'brand\

Function:
> *noun*

Etymology:
> Middle English, torch, sword, from Old English;
> akin to Old English *bærnan* to burn

Date:
> lately

1: the core of an individual's being 2: a mark that precedes or announces an individual, as if by reputation, or one that lingers or remains after that individual's departure 3: a type of energy that radiates from an individual 4: a standard by which a corporation, individual, or group of individuals looks to operate 5: a formula that takes shape when several ingredients come together in a designated way, to achieve a predetermined goal 6: the measure we make of ourselves and each other 7: a reputation, image, or marker, intended to outlast, outshine, or outperform 8: the manner or style of dress or demeanor by which an individual chooses to express his or her personality, inclination, or character

■ Daymond John's Dictionary ■

"Everyone who's ever taken a shower has an idea. It's the person who gets out of the shower, dries off, and does something about it who makes a difference."

—Nolan Bushnell
American inventor, engineer, and entrepreneur; founder of Atari video games and Chuck E. Cheese restaurants

*"I'm not a businessman.
I'm a business, man."*

—Jay-Z

Foreword

The most explosive character on the TV sensation *Shark Tank* and perhaps one of the greatest rags-to-riches entrepreneurs in this country, Daymond John, tells you how he built FUBU into one of the greatest, most successful brands in this country. John reveals how a poor kid hawking shirts and hats from a duffel bag outside of the Queens Coliseum in Jamaica, New York, grew his company into a global powerhouse, to show you how starting small can lead to scoring big. Explaining how to brand and his mantra of item-brand-lifestyle, he puts you in a position to start the next FUBU. Selfless, determined, inventive, creative, John's the real deal, the twenty-first century businessman who uses all of the new technologies, like Twitter and Facebook, to his advantage. He puts you in your own personal shark tank and will get you, with *The Brand Within*, to triumph with nothing but your wits, hard work, ethics, and street smarts. If you only read one book to help you figure out how to turn a small idea and a small amount of capital, into a household brand with an ever-broadening appeal, *The Brand Within* is the way to go.

James "Jim" Cramer
Host of CNBC's *Mad Money* and
co-founder of TheStreet.com

OPEN
Word

Confession: I don't always listen to my messages. Not exactly the best strategy, if you mean to get and keep an edge in business, but I can't keep pace. Hey, I try, but the messages pile up. My thing is, there are six or seven different ways to reach me, so if I miss you on the first pass you'll hit me back and get me the next time. Or, maybe not.

If it's important, you'll track me down. If it's not . . . well, then I didn't really miss out, right?

It's not that I'm lazy or irresponsible, or some terrible, unaccountable businessman. And it's not like I don't believe in networking and cold-calling and all that good, hustling stuff we need to do to stay out in front. It's just that each time I grab a new phone or electronic device, or sign on to a new social network or service provider, it comes with a new phone number, address, link, application . . . whatever. I get my new favorites going and they push the old ways of contacting me a little further on down the list, so now Twitter and Facebook and BBM and all my different numbers and e-mail addresses have virtually replaced all the old ways of reaching me. I still keep my business cell phone, but I hardly ever reach for it because it's not that relevant anymore. It's old school. If there's some active piece of business going on, the people I'm dealing with will have my current contact information. If there's some new piece of business flowing through my office, it'll find its way to me, too. Basically, it's the stuff from out in left field that slips past the technology overload, the calls from folks I haven't spoken to in a long time, or the ones who get one of my obsolete numbers from a friend of a friend of a friend.

Every once in a while, I'll make an effort to clear my office phone messages, but by that point there'll be a couple hundred lined up in my in-box, so I usually end up sending them to my assistant and hope she'll figure them out. On this one night, though, I was too tired and frustrated to even pass all these piled-up messages to my assistant. Mostly, they were a waste of her time, too. Took me a while to realize it, but I got there eventually. The callers were pretty much all the same: realtors, insurance agents, and stockbrokers on a cold call with a hot tip . . . one pitch after another, hardly worth the effort to hit "delete" and move on to the next one. And so I was about to erase them all, but for some reason I stopped myself and thought, *Aw, just listen to a couple.*

I don't know why I thought listening to the first few messages would make it any easier to delete the rest, but that's what I did. Told myself I'd listen to five. Like it was a "good luck" thing. Like maybe I'd turn up something worth pursuing. Sure enough, second or third message in, there was a call from Mark Burnett's office. Just hanging there, waiting for me to hit play and listen. Mark Burnett, the super-successful producer of reality television shows like *Survivor* and *The Apprentice*. The message itself wasn't too specific or too promising, and to tell the truth I didn't think a whole lot of it, but now that I'd heard it I'd follow up on it. No doubt. Why? Well, I knew Mark Burnett by reputation. I knew he made a ton of money on these shows. Most importantly, I knew and admired his brand—which to me symbolized hard work, dedication, quality, and the same entrepreneurial spirit that moved me and my boys at FUBU. Bottom line: he's a brand, so he'd get a return call.

I sent the message on to my assistant and told her to put Burnett on my call list, and then I went about my business. For all I knew, that might have been that . . . except it wasn't. The message was a couple days old by this point, but fresh enough that they were still waiting for my return call.

Turned out Burnett's office wanted to talk to me about a new reality show, based on a reality series that had been airing in Europe, Canada, and Japan. A business show, called *Dragon's Den* in those other versions, where would-be entrepreneurs came before a panel of expert investors and pitched the expert on their ideas for various start-up ventures, products, and services. It was like *Survivor*, only here these contestants were looking to survive and thrive in business, which can be a whole lot more cut-throat and brutal than a remote jungle. The payoff of the show was that if one of the experts on the panel was particularly interested in a pitch, he or she could invest in the business and have a hand in it going forward.

That's kinda hot, right?

As high concepts go in reality television, this one was right up there—and the hook, for me, was that Burnett's producers thought I might bring a kind of street sensibility to the panel they were putting together for the American version, which they were calling *Shark Tank*.

Also, pretty hot—and certainly worth a conversation.

Now, I wasn't out there looking to make my move in reality television, so it's not like this was a slam-dunk. It's not like I was desperate to be on television. And yet, in the back of my mind, I'd been thinking about finding some way to make my move from the top of the world of fashion into something new. I'd just written my first book, *Display of Power*, and after it came out I discovered how much I liked being out there, talking to people looking for a way in or up or out. I'd made a whole bunch of media appearances, and I had generated a real positive response. I liked that I had something to offer in terms of inspiring people and helping them to achieve their lifelong dreams. Didn't matter if it was a big-time book signing with people lined up out the door to meet me or a small-time appearance on some MSNBC show at six o'clock on a Sunday morning. As long as one person was getting something out of it, there was joy in it. Validation, even. I'd share my story, my strategies, my insights with anyone who cared to listen, and then I'd go out and look for another shot at more of the same.

So my first thought was that this Mark Burnett call was Heaven-sent. It's like it was meant to be, that I'd even stumbled across that message from his office, with the way I'd let all those messages pile up. I mean, who decides to listen to just five messages out of a pile-up of a couple hundred, and then finds an opportunity like this one lying in wait? The whole thing was like a giant piece of karma, wrapped in a tight ball of fate, and tossed into the air on a whim. In my head, the coincidence and serendipity just added to the inevitability of it, and at the other end I was thinking, *Okay, where do I sign?* On its own, the idea of appearing on a primetime network show that meant to highlight exciting new business opportunities and hopeful entrepreneurs had a powerful appeal. Mixed in with all this chance and karma stuff, it was even more powerful, and it fit with a whole bunch of prospects I'd been looking at outside my core FUBU business, so I was inclined to pursue it.

Still, there was some due diligence to be done. Some common sense hurdles. Some stepping back and thinking things through. See, even though a part of me wanted to be out in front, making noise, and sharing my experiences on television, I wasn't about to attach myself to some low-rent, bottom-tier effort. It made no sense to be on television, just for the sake of being on television. Truth be told, I'd been offered a bunch of opportunities in television throughout my career, but I didn't want to be one of those reality show buffoons, trying a little too hard to turn a few minutes of fame into a few minutes more. I didn't want to sign on to one of those shows that took a behind-the-scenes look at my family— only business. Plus, I didn't want to be on some backwater cable channel, chasing air time with nobody watching. Nothing against people on reality shows, but it wasn't my thing. And yet, this show seemed different. Like there'd be some weight to it. Like there'd be a chance to inspire people, maybe even make a positive dent. Come on, Mark Burnett had this tremendous reputation, and his shows were flat-out huge, so it made sense to sit down and see if there was some kind of fit.

You have to realize, I hadn't known I wanted to be a part of what Mark Burnett was doing until his office made the call, but now it was a front-and-center goal. Now the idea of working on one of his reality shows was a long-held dream I didn't even know I'd had.

First things first: they sent over a copy of the British version of the show. One of the women in my office is from England, Simone, so I asked her about it. She looked at the cover of the DVD and said, "Wow, I love this show." She also said it was one of the biggest shows in the country, which told me a lot. Then I looked it up online and saw that it was big everywhere it played. Really big.

Soon as I could, I popped the disc into my computer and

watched, and I could see right away why the format had been so successful. It was entertaining, dramatic . . . real. You had all these interesting people—creative, innovative, ambitious, regular people—hoping like crazy to interest a bunch of buttoned-down investor-types to back their businesses. Some of these people had plowed everything they had into their invention or idea, or maybe they'd been working it in a mom 'n pop way for years and years, so you couldn't help but root for them. Here in the States, it would play like a show about the American dream, so after about fifteen minutes I thought this was something I could get behind. My only concern, really, was who I'd be sitting with on the panel. I didn't want it to turn out that there was just me, with a bunch of rappers, promoting their new albums. Again, nothing against rappers (some of my best friends are rappers), but most of them are not business-men. They're not market-makers, or visionaries, except maybe in the music business. I didn't want to be a part of a show that was aimed primarily at the African-American market. That was too narrow for me. I wanted to swim in the mainstream, not in some fringe puddle off to the side.

The producers didn't know just yet who might join me on the panel, but they had some ideas. At least, they had a wishlist. First name they tossed back at me was Mark Cuban, the controversial owner of the Dallas Mavericks NBA franchise, a guy who'd made tons of money in computer consulting. Of course, Mark hadn't agreed to do the show, and it wasn't even clear if anyone had ap-proached him yet, but he was on their list. They rattled off a few other names, too, and it seemed like I'd be in good company, so we went ahead and set up a teleconference call to kick things around a little more. I had no idea who'd be on the call with me. Frankly, I was hoping to finally meet Mark Burnett and learn first-hand what he had in mind for the show, even in this once-removed sort of way, but that wouldn't happen just yet.

When it came time for the teleconference, there were six people on the Burnett side of the monitors—producers and casting agent-types. On my side, there was just me and my boy Jared, and we went back and forth for a while. One of the surprises here was that the panelists on the show were expected to put up their own money, if they wanted to back one of the contestants on the show. I hadn't counted on that. Matter of fact, I hadn't really thought things through that far, except to just assume that any investment I might make would come out of my fee for being on the show, or that it would be underwritten by the production company in some way. Now that this realism was on the table it seemed like an unworkable set-up. It made no sense, really. Guys like me, who have some success in one area, get pitched all the time on all kinds of new business deals. Every day, I get a couple calls from someone pushing some start-up venture, and 99 percent of the time they're just spinning my wheels. Ten times a week, easy, I hear from folks with their hands out, looking for a leg up. I started to think I didn't need the hassle, wasting my time in such a public way on a reality show. Even worse, the *Shark Tank* producers expected me to back these entrepreneurs with more than just my money—I'd have to put my expertise and my reputation on the line, too, pledging to do whatever I could to help each venture I supported achieve some kind of success.

Like I said, completely unworkable, so I turned the tables on these producers. Started grilling them about all the flaws in their premise. Told them there was no way they'd get a guy like Mark Cuban, who was already getting more camera time than anyone could need, to stake his money and his reputation and sign on for this particular ride. What was in it for him? More to the point, what was in it for me? Not a whole lot that I could see, and yet, I wasn't prepared to brush the idea all the way aside. The fact that Mark Burnett was behind this whole thing was enough to keep the conversation going, at least for the next while, so we talked about my concerns for the next half hour or so. I asked every question imaginable, told the Burnett people how I would set it up so they'd be more likely to attract some real quality businessmen and women to their panel. Basically, I was "sharking" them, to steal a term the producers would come to use on the show, for when their panelists really grilled an aspirant on his or her business plan.

In the end, I was only lukewarm on the prospect. The only piece that kept me interested was Mark Burnett's involvement, and me wanting to align myself with his powerful brand, although Mark didn't seem to be anywhere near the project at this early stage. Still, I didn't want to push these people away . . . not just yet. So I kind of stiff-armed them, and gave only a half-hearted commitment. Not because I was playing some hard-to-get strategy, to negotiate a good deal for myself on the show, but because I was really only half-interested.

My style is to back-off before I get too close to a deal. It's a passive-aggressive thing, I'm told. I took the same approach when I was getting FUBU off the ground, before doing our distribution deal with Samsung, and here I guess I didn't to wrap my head around a prospect before I knew if it was a good fit. It was nice to be wanted, but that didn't mean I wanted in.

A couple days later, the producers called me back. Now they really wanted me, they said. They liked how I put the screws to them on that conference call. They liked how I didn't just buy whatever they were selling, without questioning it and assessing it and poking holes in it. They said I put out the kind of healthy, plugged-in skepticism they were looking for on the show, and wondered if they could send over a contract and sign me to do the pilot. No audition. No follow-up meeting. No sit-down with Mark Burnett.

I thought, *Whoa, didn't see that one coming.*

Frankly, I could have gone either way at this point, but the idea of working with Mark Burnett was still a powerful lure. In many respects, it was the only thing this show had going for it, from my perspective. Yeah, the premise was interesting enough, and it sounded like the kind of show I'd certainly want to watch, but I wasn't hot to put up my own money to finance any of the half-baked, hair-brained pitches I knew I'd hear on the panel, same way I wasn't hot to hear those pitches in my real life, every damn day.

So I told them to send over a contract and I'd give it some thought, and when I finally got around to looking over the paperwork I realized I'd have to pass on this opportunity, no matter how much I wanted to work with Mark Burnett on a primetime network show. The problem? The contract had an exclusivity clause in it that prevented me from appearing as a regular on any other television show. This was a big-time problem, because I'd been pitched on the idea of being a sideline player on E!'s *Keeping up with the Kardashians*, as a life coach and mentor to Khloe Kardashian. She was moving to New York, and I'd already shot an episode with her, and the plan was for me to continue on in that role going forward, and to appear on another four or five episodes. All told, maybe I'd be on the air a total of ten minutes, spread out over all these shows —a nothing gig, really, but Khloe was a friend and I'd given her my word and I wouldn't go back on it for this other opportunity. Wasn't even an issue. So I sent back the contracts and explained that there was a conflict.

End of story, right? Well, not so fast . . .

Almost immediately, I got a call from Burnett's people, telling me not to worry about the *Kardashians* episode I'd already shot, as long as I didn't shoot any additional episodes—but that didn't really solve the problem. I still had that commitment I'd made to Khloe, and I wasn't about to go back on it. Didn't matter that her show would just feature me in a minor way, on basic cable, or that my footage might even wind up on the cutting room floor and never make it on the show. Didn't matter that this other show was promising me a featured role, on primetime network television. And it wasn't about weighing one against the other. It was about keeping my word, plain and simple. That's how I put it to the people in Mark Burnett's office. I said, "Thanks, but no thanks."

People thought I was crazy. For all its reach and scope, the entertainment industry is a pretty small, insular community, and word got around double-quick that I'd turned down an offer from Mark Burnett. I guess, when you're out there trying to reinvent yourself and grow your reputation as a motivational consultant and empowerment entrepreneur, the exposure that could come my way from this one show was like winning some brass ring—or, the lottery. I got a call from an agent friend, out in Hollywood, telling me I should have my head examined, for setting this opportunity aside. He said, "Daymond, I've got superstar movie actor clients who would give their right arms to be on a prime time reality show. And you're giving that up for what? Maybe four or five minutes on an E! channel show that hasn't even been picked up yet for next season?"

"It's out of my hands, man," I said. "I gave Khloe my word. Can't do anything about it."

I wasn't about to call Khloe on this, and put her in the tough spot of holding me to my promise. (Hey, she would have asked me if I'd gone crazy, too.) To me, that would have been like looking for an out, a loophole. It would have gone against the personal brand I'd spent my whole life putting together, and undermined whatever credibility and integrity I'd managed to collect along the way.

You're only as good as your word, right? With me, my word is my brand. If it gets around that I can't be counted on . . . well, then I'll never get anywhere. In life, in business, wherever. Was I crazy, to invest this tossed-off, handshake-type promise with such significance? I didn't think so. Still don't. Yeah, it meant I couldn't step up on this Mark Burnett deal—but like I said, it was out of my hands. Wasn't even an option.

All I could do was move on, and hope for the best, and know in my bones that I was true to my word. My bond. My brand. It was like that great line from *Scarface*: "All I have is my balls and my word, and I don't break 'em for no one, d'jou understand?"

Branded!

*"Next to doing the right thing, the
most important thing is to let people
know you are doing the right thing."*

—John D. Rockefeller

ONE
Here's the Deal

You are what you eat.

You are what you wear.

You are what you drive, where you live, what you drink, how you vote, what you stand for, how you love, hate, dedicate . . . you with me on this?

From the day you're born, you're branding yourself as some thing or other. You can't help yourself. Might not even realize what you're doing, even as you're doing it. Until the day you die, you'll advertise your character, your integrity, your passion, your faith, your background . . . all on the back of every choice you'll ever make as a consumer of goods and services and ideas, from the clothes you choose to wear to the person you choose to marry to the house or apartment you choose to occupy. You'll do this without realizing it, and with every intention. It will happen to you just as *you* will happen to *it*. You'll look up one day and realize you've been reshaped and reconsidered in much the same way websites like Amazon and Google can track your purchases and searches and develop a kind of user profile to help them suggest items or links that might be of interest. Every move you make will establish or re-establish your position, and shape and re-shape how the world looks back at you.

Like it or not, intentional or not, you will be stamped—branded, set off from the rest of the crowd in some distinct way, and once you've been tagged, it'll follow you around for a while.

It's not just you. And it's not just me, projecting. It's all of us, and it's all around. The first words we speak serve notice that we will not be denied. The first time we cry announces our emotions. The first time we push something or someone away, and the first time we grab at something or someone else and pull it close, we send a signal about our likes and our dislikes. The first time we stand up by our little selves, we put out a message that tells the world who we are and what we hope to accomplish and how we plan to get it done. And that's just the beginning. From there it just gets bigger and bigger. The choices we make about how we carry ourselves, the people we associate with, the way we parent, teach, or otherwise shape our children, the places we go, the politicians we support, the music we listen to, the relationships we build and the ones we tear apart . . . they all put a stamp on who we are, whether we realize it or not. (Whether we *like* it or not, as well.) It's not just about what we buy. It's what we do with what we buy. It's what we *don't* buy, too. It's what the things we buy have to say about us—what we *do* with them, how we put them on display or store them for safekeeping or keep them to ourselves. It's how we save or splurge in order to pay for the diamond necklace, the Sub-Zero refrigerator, the ultra-slim laptop we really, really can't afford but really, really can't live without.

It's the bumper stickers we put on our car—*and* the car itself. And, it's the t-shirt we buy on vacation, to tell the world where we've been.

Every time we make a purchase or a statement or some kind of pro-active move, we put out these messages and create an impression. Over time, the labels we wear begin to define us. The jewelry we display calls attention to us, just as our tattoos and piercings make their own noises on our behalf. We're packaging ourselves, and putting ourselves out there for mass consideration, the same way companies package their goods and services in all those attention-grabbing ways.

It's a cumulative thing. Every venture and adventure . . . it all adds up and starts to give us shape. Even when we guard against any kind of fashion statement, we make a statement. When we dress down, we send a branding message; when we dress up, same deal. When we "slum it" in a community beneath our means or a neighborhood about to "turn," it shouts how we want to be seen every bit as much as when we reach beyond our means, in a pricey zip code. Without really meaning to, hippies and slackers put it out there that they're untouched by material concerns—and this, too, is a kind of branding message.

When we keep quiet on an issue, or take a sideline position on a cause or a movement? Another tag on our backs.

Every misdeed and miscalculation? Those suckers add up as well. It all adds up—get it, man? That's the idea. We pile one personal choice on top of another personal choice, one impulse on top of the next impulse, until one day we're standing on top of a mountain of choices and impulses, and how we stand (and, how *high*) tells the world everything it needs to know about who we are and where we've been and what we hope to accomplish.

Okay, so that's my basic premise here—and the power of the premise is that it's just that, basic. It's fundamental, really. Don't need me to be telling you this, but I'm telling it anyway: we live in an era of brand-identity, plain and simple, and this all-out, all-over branding push has spilled over into our identity-identity. It's at the root of every transaction—social, consumer, business. It's laced into every conversation. Our point of view stamps us. Our opinions stamp us. Our experiences, too. We're stamped by what we know, and who we know and how we interact with our friends, our family, and our colleagues, and we'll do well to recognize this at every turn. Pay good and careful attention to it, because we're judged and considered by how we put what we know into play. Even the things we *don't* do, the decisions we *don't* make, the interactions we choose to avoid . . . they help to paint our picture. Every purchase we make goes into the mix of who we are. Every purchase we resist or reject or ignore completely . . . same deal.

It wasn't always in our DNA, this "brand" we all come to carry, but it's in there now, coded in such a hard-wired way that there's no shaking it off. And I'm guessing it'll be with us for a long, long time. It reminds me of how royalty can't shake itself off for trying; if you come from blue blood, you will always bleed blue blood. If you're born into a lower caste, in some societies, you will always be in that lower caste. There's no such thing as upward or downward mobility. You are what you are, branded at birth as one thing or another, and we've carried that mentality into our social brands. We've set it up so the world knows us in a certain way—by what we buy, where we live, how we dress, the way we walk, and on and on. Even our accents and speech patterns put out tell-tale signs about how and where we were raised, our level of education and sophistication, our hopes and dreams and everything in between.

There's no hiding from ourselves, I'm afraid.

Step outside or turn on the television and see if I'm right about this all-over branding business. Look around, *all* around, and see what you see. If you're not living in the middle of nowhere, you're probably being hit with logos and catch phrases and tiny parcels of common ground that are meant to connect every imaginable product to every potential consumer in every conceivable way. Hey, even if you *are* living in the middle of nowhere, you're probably caught in the same crossfire, because like I said there's no escaping it. Go hiking in one of our national parks, and you won't get more than a couple hundred feet before coming across some Thermos-toting, North Face-wearing, Range Rover-driving, Gatorade-sipping, Discover Card-wielding outdoor-type who can't help but announce himself all over the wilderness—and when he's done with his announcing he'll post his vacation pictures online in case any of us missed the point.

Once again, you don't need me to be telling you this. It's transparent, man. It's in the air and all around.

Extending the Reach

We live in a strange time, and the strangest piece is that the equation has flipped over the past couple generations. The basic transaction between business and consumer has been transformed. Maybe you didn't see it happening, but it up and happened, and it's not going to up and *unhappen* any time soon. It's a whole new world. I launched my own company in the 1990s, and even that business landscape has seen a thorough makeover. It's hard to recognize where we were not too long ago by where we are right now. To be all the way blunt about it, I don't know that I could get a business like FUBU going today, given all the new barriers to entry that have surfaced in the past few years. In just the past decade, the American marketplace has done a complete 180 on American marketers. It used to be that the tastemakers and brand-builders on Madison Avenue and Hollywood Boulevard called all the shots. They told us what to wear, and we wore it. They told us what to buy, and we bought it. They told us what to eat, and we ate it. You get where I'm going with this? Used to be pretty much a one-way street, even just a decade or so ago, when I launched FUBU, but now it cuts both ways. There's been a change, past couple years. Now we tell them what we want, and they give it to us. Now we call the shots. That's a seismic shift, don't you think?

As I write this, there's an article on my desk from a recent issue of the *New York Times*, talking about how Kellogg, the food giant, is reintroducing the Hydrox sandwich cookie—primarily because consumers wrote in and all but demanded that the company return the item to the shelves. Hydrox, for those of you with other things on your mind than sandwich cookies, was never more than a poor cousin to Oreo, even in its heyday. At least, that's how I remembered it as a kid. Now, here's what I'm learning from the article: the Hydrox cookie was introduced by a company called Sunshine Biscuits in 1908. Then, when Sunshine was sold to Keebler in the 1990s, the cookie lost some of its market share, and by the time Kellogg bought Keebler in 2003 they weren't selling enough of these puppies to continue the brand. The public perception of the Hydrox cookie had gotten a little old and tired, according to a guy named Brad Davidson, the Kellogg suit quoted in the *New York Times*.

But Kellogg kept hearing from loyal consumers, who wrote in to find out what happened to their favorite cookie, and from its own sales force, who indicated there was still a demand for the product, even in a scaled-back way. At first, those letters were coming through in dribs and drabs, but once the company started paying attention to the Internet, and set up a website with the standard interactive features, it became easier and easier for folks to reach out and speak on this. Eventually, as these tiny protests continued, the company decided to dust off this particular "ghost" or "orphan" brand, and reintroduce the Hydrox cookie in a classic, retro way, to coincide with its 100th anniversary.

Of course, it wasn't *just* that a vocal segment of the American public had the munchies for this particular cookie, but the marketing and branding experts at Kellogg must have realized that they were sitting on an untapped asset in this dormant brand, and that realization must have coincided with a shift in strategy about the sandwich cookie market in general. There was a potential profit center there they could no longer ignore, even though they'd been ignoring it for a good long while. Some experts estimate that it would take from $300 million to $500 million to recreate the level of brand awareness that exists for some of these old, familiar products, so the move made good business sense, especially as the cookie's 100th anniversary was coming around on the calendar, but I mention it here because it reflects how responsive certain companies have become to the whims of certain consumer groups.

We tell it like it is and expect to be heard.

Lift Your Voice

It's endlessly fascinating to me, the way the customer is plugged in to these companies and the way the companies are responding to that connection. There's a great example of this, which has been bouncing around the advertising community for a bunch of years, where consumers pointed out a glitch in a Tiger Woods video game put out by EA Sports, a top video game company. Some gamer posted a clip on YouTube, showing a flaw in the game that allowed Tiger Woods to tee off on a pond. That might have been the end of it, but folks caught on—and in this narrow slice of cyberspace, at least, it became a big deal. A short time later, EA Sports responded with a YouTube video of its own, claiming the pond feature was no flaw. "It's not a glitch," the ad said, referring to Tiger's ability to tee off on a water hazard. "He's just that good."

Okay, so that struck me as a pretty smart, funny, appropriate response—but the real key to understanding the current marketplace was that there was any response at all. And then, to top it off, there was a hastily produced ad from EA Sports, showing Tiger Woods in action, walking on water and approaching the tee. That's how close the connection is these days between business and consumer—close enough to generate such an intimate back and forth.

Today's consumer wants more and more to belong to a brand, a movement, an ideal, while our entrepreneurs and business leaders look more and more to tap into that ready loyalty to build recognizable, sustainable brands, to create an interactive environment and a sense of virtual community, to help launch new product lines, to reintroduce or reinvigorate tired old items or trademarks or sandwich cookies that have fallen out of favor.

Somewhere in the crunch of traffic on this two-way street lies the secret to building and sustaining a successful brand. It's not enough any more for a customer to just buy a product and be done with it. From where I sit, that kind of one-time transaction was never what the retail business was about, but these days retailers are looking for customers to buy into the whole program, long term. The one-shot deal is dead and gone. Instead, we've got our full-fledged movements up for sale, our fully-realized movies. Our life stories and long-held loyalties. Our *context*.

Yeah, you can make some money off a one-shot buy, but it's one-shot money. Who needs one-shot money when there's long-term money to be had? The idea is to build a viable, sustainable business, not some fly-by-night operation. On the flip side, who needs to make a one-shot purchase, when there's a long-term commitment to be made? That's what today's consumer is looking for, and companies need to understand this basic shift if they're looking to capture any kind of serious market share. They need to climb inside the head of the guy doing the buying and recognize that he wants something more than the instant gratification of that one purchase.

Check this out: it costs ten times more for retail businesses to win new customers than it does for them to speak directly to existing customers. And, it takes ten times more imagination to develop a customer loyalty strategy than a customer retention strategy. If you want to really bite into some market share, you've got to add value to your customers' experience. Consistently. Deliberately. Genuinely. You've got to remind yourself that folks aren't looking just to make a single purchase, not anymore. They're looking to buy into a whole program. The deal is, if they drink a certain kind of champagne one night, they'll drink it for the next while. If they drive a certain kind of car one season, they'll drive it for the next decade. And, if they like one line of your products, chances are great they'll respond to another line of your products.

Clearly, the shift in consumer loyalties has everything to do with the increasing importance of the Internet in the lives of American consumers. In the last ten years, we've become more and more connected to the companies supplying our goods and services, and I think it's fair to say that by this point every company even remotely involved in the business of selling has some type of on-line presence. This can range from a cutting-edge player like Nike, where consumers can custom design their own footwear and athletic gear, to staid, old school brands like Clorox, where loyal customers can check in and offer their thoughts on bleach and fabric softeners and all that other stuff we tend to stow under the kitchen sink without really thinking about it.

Do right by your customers this one time, and they'll do right by you the next time, and the time after that. That's the current school of thought in marketing circles. Of course, this kind of sustainable loyalty goes out the window if you start messing with it. A tainted brand—one that falls out of favor for one reason or another—can't expect to hold onto its base, so you want to make sure that your product is associated with the right movements and trends in the popular culture. You want to keep a good thing going. Play it right and your customers will follow you anywhere, as long as there's a legitimate point of connection with the core product or service that earned that allegiance in the first place. That's the message of today's consumer culture. That's the transaction we're after, the kind of relationship we all want with our customers.

It's become a long-term deal, baby, and it's up to each one of us to hold up our end.

The Things We Carry

Let's face it, we're all about the brand, and it starts with how we brand ourselves as individuals. Have you branded yourself a trustworthy person? When you walk into a room, do you make eye contact? Are you forceful? Do you speak like you're on top of your game, like you won't fall back from anybody who gets in your face and challenges you? Do you use words appropriately, or does it sound like you're trying to show off by flashing a meant-to-impress vocabulary that's clearly not your own? And what about your clothes? Do you wear tailored suits? Are there holes in your jeans? Do you do crazy things, or have a short temper? Do you dot your *i*'s with little circles or hearts or some other embellishment? Do you take the time to clip and polish your fingernails?

Do you *smell* good?

Let me spend some time on this last one, because it's telling. Better believe it, it's come down to smell. The nose knows—and it'll turn up or down on you in a whiff. Forget for a moment that we seem to want our scent to announce us in a meeting, at a club, on the street, because there's a real logic to this part of it. I mean, we don't want to *offend* anyone by smelling funky, or put out that we don't know how to keep ourselves clean and fresh. But it goes beyond that. Now we want our scent to link us in some way to someone else— someone rich or successful or glamorous or whatever. Someone who represents what we want to represent. Or maybe we want to call to mind a certain time or place or state of mind, like being out in the wilderness or in a bubble gum factory, or whatever. I'm guessing all of this is tied into our primal natures, like we're all on some Discovery Channel nature documentary, putting out these alluring scents to attract a mate, or success, or whatever it is we're looking for.

Consider the millions of dollars pumped into the celebrity endorsement end of the fragrance industry, and you'll get what I mean. Back in the day, Elizabeth Taylor was one of the only movie stars with her own perfume line, but now we've got people wanting to smell like Britney Spears, Michael Jordan, J-Lo, Paris Hilton. Burst onto the scene in some sudden, all-encompassing way, and chances are someone will try to bottle your *essence*—a sense of who you are—and sell it to your admiring fans. Hey, we even put the FUBU brand on a men's fragrance line for a while, for folks who wanted to embody the full flavor of our urban lifestyle.

I don't mean to make it personal, but it *is* personal, and as soon as we *get* that it's personal we can figure things out. We can find our way through the marketing muck and start to own it, at least a little. We can start to make it work for us, at least a little. It all comes down to packaging, and how we present ourselves is the central piece of the package. Your reputation is your base, that's where it starts, but then you build off of that when you go out to buy a watch or a new cell phone or a new fragrance. The things we buy and put to use in any kind of public way say a ton about who we are and how we want to come across. It's been a while since a nothing pair of jeans and a blank t-shirt made any kind of fashion statement—although, I guess, this too puts out an important signal. It tells the word you can't be bothered with labels or trends or falling into step with the popular culture.

It's the *anti-brand* brand, and it puts out its own signal.

Feeling "Brand-ish"

There's a phrase I toss around when I'm hanging with my crew, whenever I stumble on a course of action or a new interest or style or focus. Whenever one of us seems about to grab onto something new and make it our own. Whenever there's a movement or a moment breathing down on us and we want to be a part of it, slap a label on it, and mark it for future reference. It could be a new artist, or a new product, or a new catch-phrase that's got us all excited, in a personal way. I'll say we're feeling a little "brand-ish"—meaning that we're fully prepared to be shaped or influenced by whatever it is we're about to do or buy or say next. That we're taking note and giving notice that there's something *real* going on. Something good and right and sure. *Brand-ish*. Yeah, I know, it's already a word on its own, with no help from me, but I turn it around. I don't use it like I'm flaunting some new weapon or idea; I'm just slapping that good, 'ole "ish" suffix on the back of my brand to express that I'm feeling stamped or manipulated or advertised-to. Or, that I'm about to turn the tables and put some of that stamping or manipulating on you, like I'm jumping to announce some next big thing.

Brand-ish.

As in, brand-like. Or, leaning in a big way towards a big new idea or ideal. If we've just listened to a hot new rapper, about to burst onto the scene, we'll say we're feeling a little brand-ish, like we're about to "own" this guy and bring him into our world. If one of us comes back with a hot pair of new kicks, we can be brand-ish about that. Or, if there's some silky move we picked up on in some movie or video, and we seem determined to try it on for ourselves, . . . well, then we're brand-ish about *that*.

(Okay, so maybe I'm a little off my game in the coining-a-phrase department, but I figured it was worth a shot. I mean, marketing types are always coming up with new words and catch-phrases and slapping them on their products or concepts and hoping they stick. Don't know if that'll happen here, with all this *brand-ish* business, but I might as well push it and push it and see what happens. Can't blame a hustler for tryin'.)

Like it or not, believe it or not, embrace it or not . . . people judge you in the first ten seconds after meeting you. This is not necessarily a good thing or a bad thing, but it's very definitely a thing, and we'll latch onto it if we're smart. We'll recognize that we're feeling *brandish* when we don't even realize it. About ourselves, and about each other. We're wielding whatever it is that's got us all excited, like we're waving a flag or setting off fireworks or switching on a neon sign and telling the world what we're about. It's human nature, out in force. In a courtroom, jurors get an impression of the guilt or innocence of the defendant just by looking at him. They can't help but follow their gut, no matter how forcefully they're instructed by a judge to keep an open mind and hear all the evidence before reaching any conclusions. That's why the best defense attorneys put their clients in a suit and make sure they're clean-shaven and styled and put-together, so they don't have to work against a negative first impression.

Same goes for a company just starting out. They're also looking to hit the ground running, however they can. They're looking to make a name for themselves, an identity, to gain some kind of edge. They also care about how they "dress"—meaning, what kind of appearance they make when they step into the room, or drive people to their new website, or start airing their first commercial. That's why they put all kinds of time and expert attention into designing the right logo, the right letterhead, the right office space, the right *look* and *feel* that will mix-master together in such a way that it makes some real noise on the company's behalf.

This is the nut of today's consumer-driven brand identity movement, and it represents an important shift in the marketing of goods and services to the youth market, to young professionals, to baby boomers and to retirees—a shift we need to understand both as buyers and sellers.

What about you? Are you feeling a little brand-ish right about now? Ready to figure out a thing or two that might help you make your mark going forward? Willing to think what can happen once you start paying a little more attention to the flags you choose to wave, and the ones being waved everywhere you look? Able to use the tools of influence you wield or "brand-ish"—the media, billboards, the court of public opinion—to get your points across? Open to the all-important, all-powerful idea that just as you are being manipulated at every turn by all these businesses and corporations trying to get you to buy into whatever it is they're selling, you're out there doing some manipulating of your own?

Stay with me for these next few pages and see if you don't come out the other end knowing a little bit more about what it takes to build a brand and get people to buy into it, along with what it takes to become your own successful brand and get people to buy into you.

Why We're Here

In the end, this is not just a business book. It's not just a lifestyle book, either. And it's not one of those dry how-to type books that make you feel like you're in a classroom when you're reading it. That's not what I'm after here. What I hope to do with this book is reach out to anyone who wants to get a leg up on their own careers and move about with a little more confidence in their day-to-day lives. To take a step back from their relationships—personal and professional—and take a fresh look at how the image they put out determines their present and future path. It's a book for the business leader and for the consumer who likes to be out in front of the latest trend. It's a book for parents, looking for tools to help make their children more powerful consumers and to teach them how to build their own brands as they grow. It's a book for young adults, looking to build and sustain the personal and professional relationships they'll draw on for the rest of their lives.

And, more than anything else, it's a book meant to remind readers that they will prosper from making the right choices, from conducting themselves in the right way, no matter what stage of the business world they happen to occupy. I'll look back and offer examples from my FUBU career to illustrate certain points, and in some cases I'll look over my shoulder at what's going on in the world of fashion, or hip-hop, or entertainment in general, to help make my case.

My hope is that readers walk away from this book realizing it's not enough to talk the talk. You've got to walk the walk, if you mean to get and keep ahead. In the pages to come, we'll ask and answer one of the all-important questions of our time: are we being manipulated by all these Madison Avenue-types trying to get us to buy this or that hair gel, or this or that cologne? The short answer, for now: hell, yeah. But let's remember that consumers can also do some manipulating of their own. If you're in the public arena, you're out to win some kind of public support. Doesn't matter if you're doing the buying or the selling, the bottom line is this: virtually every business is out to build a brand, in one way or another, and at the same time they're trying to brand their customers as one thing or another. We need to understand that. We do it to each other, too, on a personal level. We're all in sales—in one way or another. We sell ourselves to our boss, to our friends and co-workers, to our families, and we need to understand this as well.

I'm not sure that knowing any of this will do us any good—best I can tell we might be powerless against the forces of marketing that have lately taken hold—but it's better than *not* knowing, don't you think?

Branded!

"We all self-conscious. I'm just
the first to admit it."

—Kanye West

JUST ONE IDEA
The Thick 'n Sweet Casebook—Vol. I

A hot idea can cover a lot of ground. It can fire up a business plan, excite potential investors, leap-frog the traditional barriers to entry in a crowded field, and crank things up in the face of established competition. It can get things moving, no question.

Conversely, a not-so-hot idea can dig a hole in the ground before you even get started. It can get you moving so far in the wrong direction that by the time you look up from all your missteps it's tough to scramble back and set things right.

In the end, it's all about execution and how you make and market your product and implement your strategy, but if your product or strategy is flawed to begin with there's not a whole lot you can do to keep things moving along. Ain't no marketing plan on this green earth that can sell fuzzy ear muffs on South Beach.

But where are all the hot ideas? How can you tell a hot idea from a warmed-over notion that's got no real shot? Those are the killer questions of our time—and the killer frustration is that there's no one set of answers. No, you've got to play your hunches—that gut feel that tells you that you might be onto something. And you've got to play them smart, and hope you don't get caught short.

I know, I know . . . this is easier said than done. If jump-starting a new business was such a no-brainer we'd all be sipping champagne and driving Phantoms. People are always coming up to me, telling me how frustrated they are that every niche, every concept, every business opportunity has been exploited into the ground. Young people especially. That's how the business landscape looks to them from their sideline perspective. They're either intimidated by it, or they think it's too easy, or they think there's nothing left for them, that the good ideas have all been picked clean. A lot of them, they see success all around and they feel like they've missed the boat, like the folks who came up with McDonald's and Microsoft and MTV have left nothing on the table for the next generation of entrepreneurs. I see their point. I get it.

To tell the truth, I felt that way too, when I was trying to get things going with FUBU. I knew clothes, and I knew how to sew, so I went with what I knew at a time when the fashion industry wasn't nearly as crowded as it is today. Also, I knew how to sell, from years of hustling product outside concerts and festivals. And so, yeah, I went with what I knew—but the reality was I didn't know a thing. I had a product and I went with it, that's all. Other than that, I was as stupid as every other kid on the street with big dreams. I was like Ralph Kramden in *The Honeymooners*, reaching for any hair-brained scheme I could find, hoping to catch any kind of break. For a time, it looked to me like there was no way in, and I thought I might end up working at Red Lobster for just short of forever.

But that's just whining, don't you think? That's just looking for excuses. If you mean to be an opportunist, you've got to be out there hustling for opportunities, not sitting on your hands at home, coming up with a sorry list of reasons why you'll never amount to much. Good ideas don't drop from the sky into your lap, fully formed. You've got to go trolling for them. You've got to consider—and, then, re-consider—every prospect. You've got to think things through, and you've got to come at those things from a different angle than anyone else. Then, if you can't find that angle right off the bat, you've got to fall back and come at it again. And, if it turns out that your hot idea is only getting you into hot water, you've got to be agile enough to shift gears and regroup.

This is the nut of today's marketplace: you've got to look at how your potential competitors are approaching their business, and develop ways to go harder. You've got to be smarter, leaner, quicker, better than the other guy. Luckier, too, but there's a whole lot more going on in the winner's circle of business ideas than simple dumb luck.

Best way to illustrate this basic truth is to just up and illustrate it. A writer friend of mine once told me to show instead of tell, so I'll set about it . . . I'll start with a story, which got me thinking along these lines. Not too long ago, a kid came up to me in a club. He'd read my last book, so he knew all about FUBU, and how I got my business started, and how I had developed a kind of Spidey-sense for good opportunities. He said, "Daymond, what can I do to get something going?"

This was a smart, ambitious kid, I could tell. He'd been to college. He carried himself well, and he knew the drill. All of the packaging pieces of his personal brand seemed comfortably in place. But what he didn't know was how to develop a concept or discover a market for himself. He couldn't get past that whining thought that all the good ideas had been taken. His interests leaned towards design and fashion, which is the way pretty much every young person I meet in the clubs tends to lean. They want music, sports, modeling, or fashion. They want what they know, I guess—but underneath all of that, some of them also want to rub up against the fame that comes in those industries. They want whatever it is they've been dreaming about; even if those dreams might be a little out of reach. They've got to figure out, do they want the glamour, or do they want to be in business? This guy seemed to want a little bit of both, which I guess was why he was reaching out to me in the first place, but I tried to get him to lean another way. I said, "Why step into such a crowded field? Why make it harder than it already is?"

He said, "That's what I know."

I said, "You don't know what you're talking about." I wasn't being hard or dismissive. I was just telling it straight. There was no reason for this kid to point down such a busy road, when he could just as easily take a back road to pretty much the same place. He didn't want to change the face of fashion; he just wanted to make a buck.

He said, "Fair enough. So tell me what I don't know."

I walked him through it. I said, "What's the best way to sell a new product?"

The kid thought about this for a heartbeat. "Sex?" he said, sort of asking, sort of confident in his answer.

"Better believe it," I said. "And does sex sell everything?"

The kid thought about this for another heartbeat, and then said, "I don't know."

If you ask me, the kid was right to hesitate here. Once again, there's no clear answer. Companies have been using hot models and suggestive scenes to sell their goods and services since the turn of the last century. It's nothing new. But what might be new here is the thought that in our enlightened, permissive society we might have finally come upon a time where sex can sell just about anything—politics, detergent, fast food . . . you name it. A couple generations back, it was probably scandalous the first time an automobile dealer used a bikini model to sell cars, or the first time someone thought to put lingerie on a live model instead of a department store mannequin. Now that kind of approach is a given, in certain segments of the American marketplace. It's almost like a default strategy. Hell, there was probably some element of sex appeal in play when John McCain reached for Sarah Palin to be his running mate. Don't go telling me that nobody noticed the Governor of Alaska also happened to be hot before they offered her a spot on the ticket.

I mentioned these things to my interested young "pupil," and together we talked it through some more. We went back and forth on this for a bit, and then we set it aside and talked about other things. At some point, the kid mentioned that his grandmother had a kick-ass recipe for pancake syrup, and right away a dozen bright light bulbs flashed in my head. That's how it is with a hot idea; it hits you before you see it coming. I thought, *Okay, now we got something.* What we had was an entry-point for an exercise in how to develop a plan of attack for a new product, and I set it out here to illustrate the promise of a new product launch—in the extreme, perhaps, but the lessons apply across the board.

Now, I don't know the first thing about syrup, and I couldn't tell you how to get this stuff into the breakfast aisle at the local supermarket if my business plan depended on it—but I do know how to make some noise and call attention to myself and whatever it is I'm trying to sell. I can shake things up, that's for sure, and that's what I set out to do here. Assuming the syrup is good enough to get folks to buy it a second time, the way in for a new syrup product could be to reach an untapped market. Think about it: who usually buys the syrup in a typical household? Probably the homemaker, right? Probably a woman. I don't mean to advance any stereotypes here, but that's just how it is. Continuing along this same line, it's a safe bet that men probably don't account for a significant percentage of U.S. syrup sales, but at the same time it's probably also a reasonable assumption that men do account for most of the U.S. syrup consumption. Young men in particular, I'm betting, because once you get older you have to worry about things like counting calories, and you stop eating heavy breakfast foods like pancakes and French toast and all that other stuff we tend to associate with maple syrup.

(Maple syrup itself, by the way, is said to be a healthier, less-fattening alternative to sugar as a sweetener, and it's actually better for you than honey, but I don't want to get ahead of myself here.)

As long as we're thinking out loud, then, let's take it as established fact that women currently buy most of the maple syrup in this country, which in turn is enjoyed primarily by young males. The hot idea here? Find a way to drive those young males into the stores to buy the syrup themselves. The way to do that? Sex, of course.

Don't know about you, but I've always been a sucker for those pictures that feature beautiful women and food. A bright red strawberry pressed against a full set of ruby red lips? Man, I'm getting excited as I write this. Barely dressed women, covered with whipped cream? That'll do it, too. It's not such a big leap, then, to hit upon the idea of slathering some pretty young thing with maple syrup, and posing her in some suggestive way. It makes a kind of perverted sense, don't you think? And it's a bulls-eye hit if you're talking about appealing to our target market. Beautiful, hardly dressed girls, slick with maple syrup, begging you to jump right in and try some. It's the American dream, right?

(One of mine, anyway.)

In this scenario, we could just as easily be selling whipped cream, or hot fudge, or chocolate milk. Honey would work, too. But let's focus on the syrup and see where it takes us. Call it "Thick 'n Sweet," and start pouring it over pretty, hardly dressed girls, and you just might be on to something. Or, maybe not. In any case, it sounds like a can't-miss marketing plan, right? Well, in the pages ahead I'll play out this loose business plan and see if it might add up to something.

For now, I'll say this: even a hot, can't-miss idea like this one can be shot through with unexpected turns and disappointments. The key is being nimble and reactive and flexible enough to take your business plan in an entirely new direction, if that's what it takes to ultimately succeed.

Read on and you'll get what I mean.

Branded!

*"Give a man a fish and he will
eat for a day. Teach a man to fish
and he will eat for a lifetime. Teach
a man to create an artificial shortage
of fish and he will eat steak."*

—Jay Leno

TWO:
The Four Stages of
Product Evolution

I'll get to how we brand ourselves as individuals a little bit later on, but let's start out on the product side of things—because that's where you'll find the beating, pulsing heart of our brand-based society. That's where we live and die and hunt and gather—in the marketplace of ideas.

I thought about this a lot as I've built FUBU: The Collection from a hand-sewn inventory of tie-top hats and high-end t-shirts to a global lifestyle brand. I built it without any kind of polished plan or MBA-type understanding of the market. All I wanted was to sell, sell, sell. I had no clear idea what I was doing except pushing ahead, making something out of nothing, going for it in whatever ways I could. It was only later, after we'd reached a certain measure of success, that I looked back and broke it down, trying to figure it all out. There are some folks who'll tell you I'm *still* trying to make sense of it all, but what I've come up with is this: in today's consumer culture, there are four stages of product evolution. Four distinct thresholds every entrepreneur must pass on his climb to the top. These four stages generally apply to retailers and to the service industry, and it's been my experience that you need to go through one in order to get to the other. We went through them at FUBU, same way every other designer, retailer, and manufacturer has gone through their version of these stages.

The four stages:
item, label, brand, lifestyle

Let's hit them one at a time: an item is an item. It's generic, no frills, like pancake batter. A book bag with no markings on it. A plastic bowl. It is what it is, and it serves a purpose. No disrespect to the folks who are out there making these items, and hustling, and trying to get ahead. They fill a need, and a lot of times they fill it well. And no disrespect to the folks who are out there *buying* these generic items, either. Maybe they're on a budget, or maybe they have an immediate need and they're out to fill it as best they can, as quickly as they can. Or maybe they just don't care about labels and lifestyles or any of that stuff. Maybe that's just not who they are.

A label is one step up from a basic item. It's something people are buying, but they don't really care what it is. It's price sensitive, like a t-shirt blank, an off-brand MP-3 player, or a flannel shirt you grab at Target or CostCo for five dollars. There's a label tucked away in there, you can figure out who the manufacturer is, but you don't care because it's not a name you know. It doesn't mean anything. It's not a name you'll reach for a second time. It's not a name you'll even remember. It's just a name. You're buying the item because of the price, because of the convenience, the look, the color, the *feel* . . . or simply because it fills a particular need at a particular time.

A brand is one step up from a label. It's where most labels want to be, at the brand level—only it takes a certain something on the advertising and marketing fronts for labels to get there. (That *certain something*, by the way, comes at a price, which of course gets passed on to the consumer.) A bought-and-paid-for brand is something that's immediately recognizable to a good amount of people. It's got an identifiable logo, a particular look, a trademark style. Here it can be about the price and the convenience, but it's also about a level of quality. A branded product is a known commodity, and whenever you wear it or drink it or drive it or plug it in, it says something about the kind of person you are—or the person you want to be. It satisfies whatever it is you need, but at the same time it helps you make an important statement. And this above all: a brand is a promise. It's a commitment, really; a seal of approval. When a customer buys into a brand, he can expect a certain level of quality, integrity, and value. It's something you can rely on, every time out.

After that, you're buying into a lifestyle. There's a promise here, too. There's that same level of trust and value and all those good things, but now it cuts across a whole line of products, goods, and services. Now you reach for a product that says even more about you because you identify with what it says about everyone else. Here again, it's a name you know and trust, reflecting a style or sensibility you want to claim as your own, but now it's bled into other areas of your life as well, beyond the initial area of perceived need. Eddie Bauer, that's a lifestyle. Nike. Tiffany. Club Med. These are companies and product lines and service organizations that start out as one thing and grow into a much bigger thing, and underneath that bigger thing is the name that started it all.

The "O" factor

Now, here's the hand-in-hand insight that goes along with these four stages of product evolution: they apply to us as individuals as well. We lift ourselves from the nondescript, huddled masses in an effort to make something of ourselves. Barack Obama, the

44th President of the United States? Perfect example. He went from being a no-frills, hard-working, essentially-unknown community organizer and public advocate—one of thousands working tirelessly and anonymously for the common good—to the most powerful elected office in the free world. But it didn't just happen. This guy didn't just burst onto the national scene, like some fully-formed phenomenon. It might *seem* that way, to a casual observer, but there was a process, an evolution. Absolutely, there was a groundswell of support and enthusiasm for this guy, but just like the word suggests, it started at the *ground* level. It was a bottom-up transformation. Back when he was a civil rights attorney, President Obama was toiling at the *item* stage of our product evolution cycle. Understand, I'm not out to diminish the good work he did in this capacity, or the good works quietly carried out by thousands of civil rights attorneys across the country, but on a global scale his work was relatively unnoticed. Yeah, he'd been editor of the *Harvard Law Review*. Yeah, he was teaching constitutional law at the University of Chicago. Yeah, he wrote a book that talked about his values and his background and all the *stuff* that went into shaping the man he had become and the vision he held for this country, even though folks weren't exactly busting through bookstore doors to buy a copy when it first came out. And yeah, he was making a local name for himself and making a difference in his community, and he surely deserved whatever props and good will came his way as a result, but if he stepped aside or moved on to something else there would have been another attorney to step in and continue fighting the same good fight.

Next, he sought election to the Illinois State Senate, representing Chicago's South Side, and here he moved from our *item* stage to a *label*. Here he announced himself as a politician, and for my money you're not a politician until you run for office. So he ran, and won, and now he stood alongside dozens of other state senators from Chicago, and dozens more across the state, with a clear and identifiable *label* on his back. Folks across Illinois might not have known who he was if they met him on the street, but Barack Obama had kicked things up a notch to where there was now some kind of marker attached to what he was doing. He filled a role, a need, a slot in the state senate. Again, if it wasn't him in that senate seat, it would have been someone else—and the majority of the good people of Illinois might never have known the difference.

A couple of years later, when he ran for Congress, he moved into *brand* territory. He didn't make it past the Democratic primary, but by now all these values and ideals we've come to associate with President Obama were attaching themselves to the man and his political career: hope, change, passion, integrity. People were starting to respond to his message, and to the quiet, silky confidence he put out when he was delivering it. Somewhere in there he caught the attention of big-time party honchos, who saw in Barack Obama a candidate who embodied these values and ideals in a fundamental way—who had been *branded* by them, really. He ran for the US Senate in 2004, winning a wide-open Democratic primary in March of that year by a huge margin, and by this point the brand was really taking shape. When he was asked to deliver the keynote address at the Democratic National Primary that summer in Boston, before he'd even been elected to national office, everything was lined up just right for this guy to kick things up yet again.

Most of us know the rest of the story. Following his 2004 convention speech, the young Illinois state senator emerged as one of the shining stars of the Democratic Party, and almost overnight it seemed he became an iconic brand. That groundswell I talked about earlier? It moved from the *ground* level to the *swelling* level, we all got caught in the rising tide, and Barack Obama came to stand for all the things the Democratic Party hoped to represent for young Americans looking to feel like they had some kind of voice in our country's future. This was especially so for young black Americans, who saw in Barack Obama a powerful symbol of opportunity, change, redemption, and hope—someone uniquely positioned to lead a kind of cultural revolution while working *within* the system.

The shift into *lifestyle* territory came quickly after that, and it really took shape when Barack Obama announced he was running for President. Now there was a real movement, and folks around the country—around the world, even—started to sign on because they were really responding to the Obama message. You started to see Obama signs and stickers all over the damn place. Not just the usual campaign signs and stickers, but symbols of hope and change that seemed to go beyond politics. These came across in campaign ads, on websites and blogs and Facebook pages and every other social networking, communication, or outreach platform available to the Obama campaign. Whatever this guy was selling, people wanted to be a part of it, and they announced their brand loyalty and their shared vision by wearing t-shirts and hats and working to get out the vote and promoting their candidate's ideals in whatever ways they could. It wasn't just about getting out the vote, although that was surely part of it. It was also about signing on and declaring your affiliation with a campaign that meant to change the face of a nation. That logo with the blue O and the ribbon of red and white stripes underneath, designed by a graphic artist named Sol Sender, came to stand for something bigger than the candidate himself, and it got to where you could slap that O on pretty much anything and people would buy into it.

It was a curious coincidence that Pepsi changed its logo around this time—its first new logo in nearly seven years, and its 11th in the beverage company's 110-year-history. But I have to think it was just that, a coincidence. True enough, the new logo featured a free-flowing white band in the middle of the Pepsi "circle," all of it done up in red, white and blue and calling to mind the ubiquitous O, but of course a giant corporation like Pepsi could never be agile enough to make such a major shift in its logo, to capitalize on the patriotic themes of the Obama campaign. A move like that takes months and months, although it certainly didn't hurt that the company's new "look" matched up so neatly with a political brand that was sweeping the nation.

Anyway, you could chant the "Yes we can!" mantra of the Obama campaign, and in it hear the rallying cry of a movement, a nation, a *lifestyle*. "Yes we can!" We'd hear it over and over again, to where it went from being a call to action to a rallying cry to an affirmation. After a while, the O alone was enough to get the man's point across—so much so that in the week following his election, *The New Yorker*, the respected mainstay of the New York literary community, highlighted the O in its name on the magazine's cover over a simple illustration of the Lincoln Memorial to signify the historic moment.

That just about said it all.

And so, in the space of one presidential election cycle, you had an unassuming local politician pinch the initial O from another icon of the African-American community (sorry, Oprah!), and write his way into American history. It was a full-on movement, and on the back of it we managed to elect the first black president in our nation's history, but it happened in this methodical way, one stage at a time.

King of Pop Culture

Timing is everything in the *item-label-brand-lifestyle* business, and this is illustrated in a big way with the sudden passing of Michael Jackson. I'm not out to beat on this great artist's reputation after he's gone, but even Michael's friends and family will cop to the fact that he went through some rough patches in his life before he died in June 2009 at the age of fifty. He went back and forth between so many highs and lows it's like he was on that rollercoaster he used to keep at his Neverland ranch, and it just so happened that he was on an upswing when he checked out. In fact, judging from the rehearsal footage we all saw in *This Is It*, the well-received documentary about the build-up to his final tour, it looked like Michael was back at the top of his game.

A side note: I was so moved by Michael Jackson's death that I wrote about it on my blog. I had some thoughts on Michael that didn't seem to fit anywhere else. "At first," I start out, "I was going to write my column on the amazing accomplishments Michael Jackson achieved during his brief life. I was planning to do this in an effort to educate the younger generation about why Mike was way more than just a singer and the reason the world is so stricken by the loss. Those who seek true power should take time to research and educate themselves on one of the last living legends this generation will ever see. I'm going to take it a bit further and talk about something else. As I try to wrap my mind around how to express in words what we are experiencing with the loss of this complex individual, I begin to understand that Michael was way more important in our lives than we have ever realized.

"This man was clearly the most recognizable face on the planet. Mike made us laugh, cry, fall in love, get over heartbreaks, wear weird clothes, get our freak on, and dance the night away! He made us dream of far-away places; he scared us with zombies; he made us face the truth about those who are poverty stricken; he tried to save the planet and teach us that race is not black or white. He gave us a peek into an extravagant lifestyle of wealth, set records that other artists will forever attempt to break, created a standard of excellence in performance, showed us the face of unhappiness with the lengths to which he went under a knife, and generally made us question the price of fame.

"He was the butt of our jokes. He made us question if we should trust our kids with those we admire. He made us value the importance of having a childhood, as we witnessed his anguish at having his snatched from him. He was the person at whom we could all point our fingers.

"Forget the saying 'I want to be like Mike,'" I conclude. "When it came to Michael Jackson, it was 'I have a piece of Mike!' There are very few people on this planet that don't have a piece of this man in their lives, whether by picture, song, article of clothing, or the way he affected their environment and the music and entertainment they enjoy today. To an entire generation (and to the entire world for many, many years), Michael Jackson was EVERYTHING. And after all of that, once the dust settles, we will go on with our lives as if he was never here. Of course, we won't forget him. The music will live forever. But that feeling we had when he was on top of the world, or that feeling we had at his immeasurable lows . . . where will those feelings go? At the end of the day, all that are left will be the songs future generations will dance to . . . or maybe not. After all, how often do we dance to the music of a previous generation?

"All of which takes me to this key question: How does a person who means EVERYTHING to us also mean NOTHING at the same time? I caught a post on Twitter that summed it up in just a few words: 'We enjoyed Michael's life more than he did.'"

That's how his life and death touched me at the time of his passing, and I put it out there for all to see, but now, all these months later, I'm still thinking about it. His passing is illustrative, I think, and certainly relevant to our branding discussion. Look back at Michael's brilliant career, and you'll see that he went through each of these basic stages on his way to the iconic "King of Pop" status, first with his brothers, and later on by himself. *Item, label, brand, lifestyle* . . . just like any other product or phenomenon. All these years later, it feels like Michael magically burst on the scene as a fully formed, fully realized entertainment giant, but of course, that's not how it happened. He went through the motions, the same as everyone else. He went from being a talented little kid who could blow—an *item*—to a reliable, relatable, remarkable piece of the Motown machine that defined a certain scene and sound for so many of us at the end of the 1960s, the *label* period for the Jackson 5. From there, with a series of hits and breakthrough appearances on shows like *American Bandstand* and *Soul Train*, Michael and his brothers became a certifiable brand. (Hop onto eBay and you can still find a Jackson 5 lunchbox from that period, so you know these kids were making some serious moves!) By the time Michael's great *Off the Wall* and *Thriller* albums seeped all the way into our national consciousness, with those trademark videos and bass lines and dance moves, it was *lifestyle* timebig time, all the time, for *all* time.

Now, it's possible to look on Michael Jackson's life and career as an *item-label-brand-lifestyle* transformation in the extreme, but the compelling piece here is how he'll be remembered in the future. Like I said, Michael had some tough times, and as I write this it's probably a little too soon to assess what his enduring legacy might be, but there's no denying that in the days and weeks following his death he was placed on the kind of pedestal we don't often see for our cultural icons. And it all had to do with *when* he died, don't you think? I mean, if Michael's untimely death had occurred when the storm of controversy surrounding some of his questionable behavior was at its loudest, he might not have been treated as such a beloved or tragic figure. His memory might have been permanently tarnished—or at least painted in some lastingly negative way. We tend to think of this type of brand progression as a forward-going process, but there's some back-and-forth to it, too. Yeah, the *idea* is to move forward, to grow the public perception of whatever it is you're doing or making or selling in such a way that you make more and more of a dent in the consumer consciousness. But that's not always how it goes, and Michael Jackson stands as a powerful illustration of the ephemeral nature of the brand growth cycle.

Surely, if Michael's death had come at a different time, his memory might not have been so warmly or overwhelmingly embraced by so many different people, all over the world. Just as surely, there'd be no denying his gifts or his genius. But if things had played out another way, there might not have been any denying or setting aside of the controversy, either. And if he had lived to a ripe old age, never again reaching the heights he'd achieved as a young superstar, it's possible his memory might have simply faded to where his passing would have made hardly a ripple on the world stage.

Something to think about.

The great lesson of Michael Jackson's life and death is this: our legacies can be flash-frozen, trumped up, and highlighted by timing and circumstance. You can be seen one way one moment and another way the next and a whole bunch of different ways after that, but it's the last picture that tends to stick.

No question, Michael had been a great big deal for more than four decades. No question, his planned comeback could have been a great success, and Michael could have returned to the public stage bigger and better than ever. He was primed to be a great big deal all over again. But he hadn't been too current or relevant in a long while, and he'd fallen from grace and out of favor along the way. The fact that he just happened to check out at the front end of all those London concert dates, at a time when we were apparently ready to forgive or look past his failures and celebrate his accomplishments, set things up in such a way that Michael left us in a freeze-frame moment, thereby assuring that his enduring legacy, his music, his signature style and his boundless talents will be allowed to live on in the ways he enjoyed when he was at the very peak of his career.

The Bottled-Water Transaction

If the President Obama and Michael Jackson analogies don't cut it for you, another way to bring these four stages down to some understandable size is to look at one particular product, in one particular industry. Take bottled water. Doesn't get much simpler or more straightforward than that. The *item* itself is plain water. You can drink your fill for free from any kitchen faucet or water fountain—and in New York City, we've got some of the best, cleanest, most purified tap water in the country. And yet for some reason we've decided we want to pay for this stuff, as much $50 for a super-luxury bottle of Bling H_2O, the highest of high-end brands that comes in a limited edition, corked, frosted, and supposedly reusable glass bottle decorated with Swarovski Crystals.

(Talk about extreme marketing concepts!)

The folks at National Public Radio ran a blind taste test, pitting Bling H_2O and a moderately priced bottled brand against New York City tap water, and the results were all over the place. Customers couldn't tell the difference among the three, which illustrates in fairly certain terms that it really is about the label, the status that attaches to certain "designer" water purchases, more than it is about taste or quality.

At the low end, you can find basic bottled water on the shelves of most discount stores or local supermarkets, often with the words "Bottled Water" as the only distinguishing marker on the label. Like I said, that's about as clear cut as it gets, right? I know, I know . . . it's available every day right in your own home; you can draw it from your kitchen sink at any time. You can find some stream and drink all you want, or stick your head out the window when it rains and suck in what you can. But now we've put the water in a bottle and slapped a price tag on it. Now we've made you thirsty when you're away from your kitchen sink, and nowhere near a fresh-water stream. Now we've got you reaching for your wallet instead of a water fountain. That's the power of marketing, the way corporations can get you to buy the stuff you're used to getting for free—whether it's for 50 cents a bottle or $50.

It's like my mother used to say, "One day the white man will figure out how to sell you air." She was right about that. (As long as I'm on it, here's one thing you need to know about my mother: she's right about most things.) Walk past an oxygen bar in any high-end mall or department store in the country, and you'll see that she was dead right.

At the *label* level, it's possible to find bottled water from companies you've never heard of, like Hilltop Falls or Mineral Valley. The idea is to attract the eye of a thirsty customer, and get him or her to think the water comes from some clear mountain spring and that it's probably a notch or two better than the stuff that comes in the unmarked or hardly marked bottles. This may or may not be true, by the way, but that's not the point. Some of this stuff is bottled straight from New York City tap water, but people are buying the convenience as well as the *idea* of a pure drinking experience. The one-time Mineral Valley consumer is not likely to seek out this brand a second time, or even remember the name on the label after the bottle has been discarded, but it serves its purpose for the time being. It satisfies a thirst.

One price point above, you'll find a familiar *brand* of bottled water, like Poland Spring or Evian. Here, too, there might be no fundamental difference in the product itself, but the name or logo or distinctive packaging might make it stand out in a crowded field.

Maybe you'll be attracted to a water bottle shaped like a flask, or one with an easy grip so you can hold it while jogging, or a flip-top sport cap. Maybe you'll like the wide-mouth opening, so you can refill it easily and use it again. Maybe you'll recognize the brand Aquafina alongside all the no-name bottles when you open the refrigerator at the convenience store. Maybe you'll remember a commercial you saw on television, where some hot, hard-bodied swimsuit model was satifsying her thirst in a hot, hard-bodied way, and somewhere in the back of your mind it registers that maybe this particular brand of bottled water will be your ticket to *that*. Maybe it's just a sweet label that catches your eye. A consumer might pay a little bit more for a bottle from a known manufacturer, or be a little more inclined to reach for a recognizable brand, even if it's a discount brand like CVS.

Now things get a little interesting: the brand-based customer will likely return to make a subsequent purchase under similar circumstances—and here for the first time on my little flow chart of product evolution you've got that all-important taste of customer loyalty. If all goes well with this first purchase, if the water does its thirst-quenching job and the price is about right, you'll be likely to look for this brand next time out.

At the *lifestyle* level, we can look to several designer or boutique brands that have branched into other items beyond their core product line. The Vitamin Water line of products is a good example —a product that differentiates itself from its competitors with distinctive flavoring that at the same time promotes good health in a variety of forms. In addition to the bottle of water itself (in this case, the bottle of *flavored* or *enhanced* water), you can also buy a t-shirt or a reusable water bottle or an energy bar that in addition to fulfilling its own need also brands the consumer as someone who buys in to the message behind the brand. For a while, you got some of this same, lifestyle experience with Perrier, which marketed a whole line of related (and, hardly related) products—like visors, coolers, and beach umbrellas.

And, up in that rarified air of Bling H_2O, you'll also make that not-so-subtle shift into lifestyle territory, where you can now buy all kinds of Bling merchandise, from ball caps to beachwear, all of which sells the image of success and luxury and looks to (loudly!) celebrate the crystal-studded good things in life, no matter the cost.

The Ultimate

These days, my favorite illustration of the *item-label-brand-lifestyle* progression can be found in the ring. Specifically, in the UFC— the Ultimate Fighting Championship ring. If you're not hip to the UFC, it's an organization that in just about fifteen years has come to control more than 90 percent of the mixed martial arts industry. It's big business, with lifestyle-level tie-ins in video games, t-shirts, concert, and promotional events. These guys came out of nowhere and created this huge space, mixing elements from all these different fighting forms. The organization is run by a guy name Dana White, and it puts fighters from all disciplines together in the same ring—a genius concept that goes all the way back to some of those stupid, cartoon-inspired arguments we used to have as kids. You know, where we sat around and wondered if Mighty Mouse could beat Superman in a fight. Well, here the promoters help us answer other pressing questions, like can a boxer beat a kickboxer? Can a sumo wrestler beat a black belt in Jiu-Jitsu? And on and on.

What's great about these fights is that there was something very generic about them to start—something very primal, almost. They were an *item*, in that they were just a way for some promoter to make a buck by pitting two guys against each other in a ring, and allowing us to watch them beat down on each other in a no-holds-barred way. If it ended there, it still would have been a money maker, but as these bouts got more and more attention, people started to look for them by name. Organizers started to put in rules and regulations, to keep the free-for-all aspects of these contests from getting out of hand. And, at the other end, the organizers had stumbled on the perfect "sport" for television. Man, I just love watching these fights! And I'm not alone, apparently. Very quickly, these fights moved from *item* to *label* to *brand*, and the UFC organization developed a rabid following, as fighters and gym rats around the world looked to step up their training in an effort to compete on this new stage.

Along the way, through its development, Dana White became a very powerful and influential figure within the UFC, eventually controlling the fates and fortunes of all these fighters coming up through the ranks. He was kind of like Vince McMahon of the WWE, only more so. If Dana White liked you, he'd keep setting you up with marquee UFC fights. If he didn't, for whatever reason, you were out. And it's not like there was any place else you could go, to fight on some other circuit. It was the UFC, or bust; it was his way, or no way.

Now, just to put it out there: I'm a fan. In a big way. Why? Well, it's the fastest growing sport in the world, and I'm on it. Very quickly, it's become a lifestyle for its fans … like me. There's a spin-off reality show, called *Tap Out*, which in turn has spun off its own clothing line, also called *Tap Out*, in addition to a whole other clothing line, called *Affliction*, which just about every ultimate fighter seemed to be wearing for a time. (Hey, they stole a page from our FUBU playbook with this one, but it's all good.) There are video games and all sorts of ways to associate with the brand online. There are UFC or "Ultimate Fighting" parties in clubs around the country, usually tied in to some pay-per-view event or other, and you can't walk the beach down in Miami or out in Santa Monica without seeing some musclehead in a UFC tank-top or visor.

Not too long ago, I was out in Vegas at a UFC fight, and the buzz around the ring was all about a rival league, which promoters were calling World Extreme Cage Fighting—WECF, for short. Here the emphasis was on grappling and street-fighting techniques. NBC TV came up with its own version, to compete with the UFC brand, but Dana White and his crew were first to the gate on this, so most people know these types of fights by his brand. The UFC doesn't have any kind of chokehold on the fights themselves, and other promoters can weigh in and stage bouts of their own, under some other banner and some other set of rules, but the folks at home tend to see these fights as UFC-sanctioned events, which at the other end means the UFC just destroys any attempts by its competitors to battle its brand. These other guys, they've got no shot, because Dana White has done such a good and effective job that he "owns" the space.

I look on at home, or in the arena, and marvel at the ingenuity of the enterprise. There's nothing really new and improved here, except for the way these fights been packaged and presented as new and improved. For years, you used to see kickboxing-type events on television, or K-1 fighting, but nobody really paid attention until the UFC, so it makes sense that they kind of own the space. They changed things up, made everything a little more contemporary, put in an octagon-shaped ring and all these other cool elements. They developed their own superstars, like Rampage, and mixed aspects of boxing with professional wrestling to create a whole new environment.

People responded to it—so much so that other folks started jumping on the same bandwagon.

The UFC promoters took something generic, put a label on it, and promoted the hell out of it until it became a brand. Then one day they looked up and it was bigger than they could have ever imagined.

One Step at A Time

Item, label, brand, lifestyle . . . it doesn't matter what you're selling, you can't get to one stage in the development of your product or service without getting through the one before. Doesn't matter what you're buying, either. The equation holds in just about every retail and service segment, and it follows us into our personal lives as well. Take a look around your house right now and you'll see what I mean. That Victoria's Secret teddy you got your lady for Valentine's Day? Think back on that. Think where it came from. At one point, it was just a basic undergarment. Then someone slapped a label on it, and after a while that label started to mean something. After a while, after a whole bunch of creative marketing and pro-vocative catalogue designs and fashion shows, that label has become a brand.

In some ways, the rise and revising of the Victoria's Secret brand was a lot like the evolution of the *Sports Illustrated* swimsuit issue—an annual event put out by a weekly sports magazine that had nothing to do with sports. Dress it up however you like (or, *undress* it, I guess), and it still doesn't fit in a publication devoted to sweat and effort and competition. But over time these swimsuit issues became so popular and so ubiquitous that any time a pretty girl stepped onto a crowded beach wearing a hot new design, people would say she could be a *Sports Illustrated* swimsuit model. Her appearance had nothing to do with the athletes who regularly graced the magazine's cover, but if everything to do with the lifestyle brand the magazine had created. And, once they put it out there and it caught on, it quickly became the gold standard, and just on the back of this one-time editorial shift the entire *Sports Illustrated* brand began to change from a weekly magazine for rabid sports fans to a lifestyle label celebrating sports, fitness, and clean, healthy living.

The Victoria's Secret brand enjoys such tremendous success that it too is a full-fledged lifestyle. Now, if you're looking to buy something for your lady to lounge around in, you think Victoria's Secret—or Vicky's, as my peoples would say. It doesn't have to be lingerie. It doesn't have to be sexy. It can just be basic flannel pajamas, or fluffy slippers, or a terry cloth bathrobe. Perfume, too. You can actually *smell* this company. They've got skin products and beauty products. It's all about the bedroom. They own that space. But it's not the same bedroom they started out in. It's not down and dirty. It's clean and wholesome and comfortable. Hey, it's sexy, too, but that's just a part of it. Now it can be a smell that calls the company to mind, or that picture of an angel they've got on most of their packaging, or a hot, beautiful image of a woman in a lace teddy. They've got it all covered. That's what you get in extreme success in the retail business. You get a much bigger space to roam around in and sell your stuff.

Of course, Victoria's Secret is just one example of this phenomenon. You see it across the board, whenever a brand becomes so big it overtakes the entire product category: iPod, to describe any MP3 player. (Before that, it was the Walkman, Sony's portable tape player, which became the default name for any personal listening device.) Xerox, to describe any copier, or even the act of making a copy. Coke, to describe any cola product. And on and on.

Get there first, like Dana White and the UFC, and you can *own* the space. Come in second and you'll be playing catch-up. Enter the field when there's already a clear winner and you might as well stay home.

Branded!

*"A market is never saturated with
a good product, but it is very quickly
saturated with a bad one."*

—Henry Ford

THREE
The Power of the Personal Brand

Okay, so it's not only about products. And it's not only about presidential candidates who transcend the political campaign and come to represent their very own movement, or bigger-than-life pop icons that fall from grace and then leave us suddenly while they're trying to pick themselves back up and reposition, re-imagine, and reinvent their tarnished brand. It's also about individuals, personalities, reputations.

It's about *us*.

Let's start at the top and work our way down: long before Barack Obama came to symbolize hope and change for America, there were other leaders who were known for one thing or another. Ronald Reagan was all about strength and patriotism. John F. Kennedy symbolized youth and vigor and courage. Martin Luther King, Jr.—equal rights, civil rights and doing the right thing. Abe Lincoln was known for his integrity. George Washington, too.

That story about George Washington, cutting down the cherry tree? ("I cannot tell a lie?") It's been told and retold by generations of grade school children all over the country, and in that one tagline is everything we needed to know about the father of our country.

Not *brand-ish* enough for 'ya? Well, let's fast-forward to some fresh examples from the world of politics—specifically, to the tar-

nished images of a few of our recently "fallen" governors. In the space
of a bad, sad headline, their reputations went from glowing to desperate. It's like an outbreak, man: South Carolina governor Mark San-
ford, torching a promising political career on the back of a bizarre,
inexplicable, and ultimately self-destructive affair with an Argentine
mistress. Illinois governor Rod Blagojevich's bizarre, inexplicable,
and ultimately self-destructive move to peddle a Senate appointment.

The Eliot Spitzer brand? I'll spend a little more time on this
one, because it blew up in my backyard—and for a while it was all
anyone could talk about in and around our offices in the Empire
State Building. As the New York State Attorney General, Spitzer
cast himself as the champion of the little guy, the watchdog of the
public good. When it was going good for this guy, he had a ton of
support, across the state—even across the country. He prosecuted
cases of white-collar crime and insider trading and basically took on
every type of corruption and scandal you can imagine, eventually
building up such a positive base that he was elected Governor of
New York in November 2006. People started talking about him like
he just might be the next President of the United States. They saw
Eliot Spitzer as a real crusader for truth, justice, and the American
way—like Superman in a pinstriped suit. That was his brand, until
he got caught in a high-end prostitution scandal and had to leave
the Governor's mansion in shame, a little more than a year after
taking office. His political career was in ruins. His marriage, too,
I'll bet. It wasn't just that this guy got caught going to a hooker that
cost him his career and his reputation; it was that his actions were
so completely opposed to the principles on which he'd built that
reputation. It was that his moral compass turned immoral when
he thought no one was looking. Who knows, maybe if it was a less

moral, less high-minded politician who got caught stepping out, he might have kept his job.

On the flip side of the Eliot Spitzer brand was the call girl caught with her legs wrapped around the governor: Ashley Dupree. Same transaction, but hers is a whole different story. Ashley Dupree brought her own baggage to the headlines—first as a teenage runaway, then as a struggling young singer, and ultimately as a high-priced call girl catering to rich and powerful clients. It's a familiar story, I'm sorry to report, but it took a weird turn when it bumped into the governor's story. Here the Ashley Dupree "brand" got painted and tainted by the brush of the Elliott Spitzer brand, and it shifted with each revelation about the case, until ultimately she was cast as a kind of victim by the tabloids—and that's where she stayed on the social spectrum, at least for the next couple months. People started listening to her music, although I'm guessing it wasn't very good because they stopped listening soon enough. And some months after the scandal, she turned up on television in a much-publicized Diane Sawyer interview, in which she came off as an apologetic girl-next-door. She reinvented herself a few times on the back of Spitzer's shame.

Obviously, this kind of personal brand is not limited to elected officials or spiritual leaders or high-priced call girls. It reaches into our mainstream popular culture as well. Remember Evel Knievel? When I was growing up, this guy was out there jumping over buildings and across canyons and doing all kinds of wild stunts, but he was doing these things as an entertainer. Somewhere along the way, he became a commodity, a brand—the Michael Jackson of his particular slice of the entertainment world. I can't say for sure whether old Evel figured this out for himself ahead of time, for his Knievel self to come across in just this way, but after a time he was as much of a product as he was a stuntman. He wasn't merely selling tickets to these extreme events, or hoping to line up some lucrative sponsors, he was selling an *image*. He was selling himself.

Evel Ways

Over time, Evel Knievel became so popular it got to where you could go up to one of your boys and say something like, "Oh, I'm gonna pull an Evel Knievel," and he'd know right away you were thinking of doing some kind of daredevil stunt. Among us kids, it became a kind of brand name for reckless, fearless behavior, and this guy was smart enough to know that and to play into that. You never saw Evel Knievel out in public without one of his flamboyant motorcycle suits. You never saw him doing something simple or sensible, like mailing a letter or eating a sandwich. That wasn't what he was about. He was all about doing those stunts, and risking his life, and pushing the envelope, and that's what filtered through.

Understand, Evel Knievel was just one guy, doing his thing and cutting his own path, but it wasn't until he died in November 2007 at the age of 69 that I started to think about his life in this type of branding context. Once I did I realized he was in good company, right up there with other visionary-types who cut their own paths to the top. Donald Trump. Michael Jordan. Hillary Clinton. Al Gore. Oprah, Tyra, Madonna, and just about every one-named celebrity you can think of. These are just a few of the icons on our current cultural landscape who appear to stand for something bigger than themselves. And, to stand *apart*. Alone. They started out representing one thing to one group of people, and ended up representing a whole bunch of other things to a whole bunch of other groups of people, and no one else was able to do quite what they were doing, in quite the same way, with anything close to the same level of success. In each case, I have to think these people have blown all the way past whatever hopes and dreams they had as young journalists, models, athletes, and singers just starting out, as they built themselves into endlessly recognizable and sustainable human brands—alone at the top of their fields.

Lately, I've been fascinated by the life and career of Bruce Lee, the American-born fighter, philosopher, screenwriter, and acting legend who almost single handedly created a film genre and a worldwide interest in the martial arts. As I write this, I've been watching and re-watching a great History Channel documentary on Lee's life and career called "How Bruce Lee Changed the World," and it's astonishing how much this man accomplished in such a short stretch of time. (He only made five movies in his lifetime, including the classics *Fists of Fury* and *Enter the Dragon*.) He didn't set out to become a cultural icon, but that's what he became.

Here's a guy who became an internationally iconic figure, in an arena he basically invented. You look at a legend like Bruce Lee, who breezed past my *item, label, brand, lifestyle* markers in no time at all and quickly emerged as an emblem of Chinese national pride, and you can't help but wonder what the rest of us are doing with our time. This guy had his hand in everything—in a full-on, all-out way. He developed his own martial arts discipline. He pioneered various body building and weight-training techniques that were considered unconventional and *out there* in his time. One of my favorites was the way he toughened up the skin on his fists by thrusting his hands over and over into a bucket of gravel and sand. (He did this five hundred times a day!) He choreographed his own stunts and fight scenes in his movies—and then, for good measure, he directed the movies, too. He didn't set out to do any of these things, but he grabbed at every opportunity. He was even one of the first to start drinking blended fruit drinks and dietary supplement to enhance his physique and training, all while he was building this great legacy with his movies. A lot of people don't know about this last part, or maybe they've forgotten about it over the years, but Bruce Lee was really out in front in the areas of physical fitness and total conditioning. He was one of the first well-known athletes to publicly embrace the benefits of a healthy diet, and you could really see the pay off because, most of the time, he was running around without his shirt on.

His untimely death at the age of thirty-two and at the peak of his many-sided career meant his brand would live on and remain a part of our life and lifestyles for generations—in much the same way Michael Jackson's legacy couldn't help but endure because of his sudden passing.

After all, it's not just how you *arrive* on the scene that sets you up on the public stage—it's also how you *leave*.

The Tiger Deal

As I write this, there's another iconic personal brand unraveling on the public stage: Tiger Woods, who went from being the best golfer on the planet, a guy who could do no wrong on the endorsement and public-speaking circuit, to someone who can't stay out of a Chris Rock punch-line about infidelity.

Now, I'm not out to mess with someone's private life. That's for the tabloids and the bloggers. Truth is, I've got no idea what

Tiger's been up to, or what was going on with him and his wife, but what seems like fair game here is taking a moment to reflect on how Tiger's reputation took such a swift hit when the news broke about his extramarital affairs. He went from a perch at the top of the world, where he could do no wrong, to the lowest of the low, where a lot of folks started wondering if he could ever set things right. It reminded me of the hit Kobe Bryant took when he was charged with sexual assault back in 2003. Now, let's be clear: Tiger wasn't charged with any crime here, and as far as I know he isn't guilty of anything except for stepping outside his marriage a bunch of times, but there are a lot of similarities, just the same. Back in the day, Kobe was like an endorsement god: Nike, Spalding, Coke, and on and on. Tiger, too, was raking it in on the endorsement front: Nike, Buick, Gillette. For a while, it looked like Kobe would never be able to get his game back off the basketball court. On the court, he was doing just fine, playing at a high level, winning championships and setting all kinds of individual records, but in the court of public opinion he was really hurting for a while.

That's where we are right now with Tiger Woods, as I send this book off to the publisher. No one can say for sure how things will shake out for him, but after just a couple of weeks, a lot of companies started dropping him as a spokesperson. They didn't want their product, and their service, their brand associated with a married man who was stepping out with all these women. I get that. I'm sure even Tiger gets that. It'll take a good long while for the dust to settle and for Tiger to remake his game and his reputation, but until that happens we can look back and see how things were. Up until this story broke, Tiger stood before us as the pinnacle of the personal brand. He went through all those stages along the way—*item, label, brand, lifestyle*—from being just a talked-about little kid golfer to winning some tournaments to making and cementing a name for himself to lending that name to products and projects that had nothing at all to do with golf. By some measures, he'd even surpassed Michael Jordan as the most beloved, most recognizable, most idolized figure in the history of sports. He was the first athlete to earn more than $1 billion dollars in lifetime endorsement deals—and that's the kind of serious paper that only comes your way if you've really got it going on. He stood for integrity, determination, and excellence. And then, all of a sudden, he didn't.

In some ways, you can even find parallels in the life and career of an athlete like Muhammad Ali, the greatest boxer of his generation, who slogged through his own controversy when he joined the Nation of Islam and later when he refused to serve in Vietnam. He went from being this larger-than-life superstar as a young Cassius Clay to being a vilified, ostracized outcast, but then he fought his way back. Same thing with Kobe. He fought his way back and outperformed everybody else and eventually all the controversy just died down. These two cats were so good, so far ahead of the field, that they just shut people up. Maybe that's how things will go down with Tiger, in the long run. Maybe he'll get back to doing what he does best, playing the best golf on the planet, and after a while folks will just forget these current difficulties and move on. Or maybe they won't forget, but they'll let these transgressions slide, and Tiger will get his life back, and his career, and his record-breaking endorsement deals.

Like I said, it's too soon to tell—but it's not too soon to wonder.

Are There Really
Cheeseburgers In Paradise?

Another example, just to show how the *item, label, brand, lifestyle* stages can be applied to an individual, and how a kid from Hollis, Queens, can reach beyond his comfort zone to make a point: Jimmy Buffett. Not *Warren* Buffett, the legendary investor. *That* guy deserves all the love—definitely, he is gangsta—but he doesn't exactly fit in this discussion. (Check that: he *does*, only that's not where I'm going in these next few pages.) No, it's *Jimmy* Buffett who gets respect here, the laid-back singer-songwriter with the carefree persona, even though I'd never really heard of him until I started researching this book. I probably caught some of his songs on the radio, but that's about it. This is the guy who had a monster hit song in the 1970s called *Margaritaville*, which best I can tell was about drinking margaritas in some tropical paradise.

Now, I'm sure Jimmy Buffett will forgive me if the song managed to pass relatively unnoticed in my neighborhood when I was a kid, but check out what this cat has built on the back of that one hit song. He's written a bunch of best-selling books. (Get this: he's one of only *seven* writers to hit the number-one spot on the *New York Times* fiction *and* non-fiction best-seller lists.) He's got a line of frozen foods, Jammin' Jerk Shrimp and Captain's Calamari Strips, with annual sales of more than $10 million. He makes and markets his own blenders, complete with several varieties of tequila and drink mixes, with annual sales of more than $9 million.

There's even a chain of successful "Cheeseburger in Paradise" burger joints, named for another one of Jimmy Buffett's hit songs, which he opened in partnership with Outback Steakhouse, and a "Margaritaville" hotel and casino in Biloxi, Mississippi, which he's building in conjunction with Harrah's Entertainment. And just for kicks, he's lent his name to a line of "Margaritaville" deck shoes and flip-flops that have quickly become one of the most popular men's casual footwear lines in the country.

Not bad for a guy with a guitar, huh?

On top of all that, Jimmy Buffett continues to tour before sold-out crowds in stadium-sized venues all around the country, and he's got his own record label as well. According to *Rolling Stone*, Jimmy Buffett's 2006 estimated earnings of $44 million placed him solidly in the top ten for all musicians. Not bad for a singer-songwriter-turned-best-selling-author-and-enterprising-merchandiser   who couldn't really catch a break when he first moved to Nashville in the 1960s. Even after he'd managed to record an album or two, he was still playing for loose change on the streets of New Orleans and down in Key West.

You chart the progression of Jimmy Buffett's life and career, and it makes you think about your own life and career. It pushes the question: where are you now? This is where the *item, label, brand, lifestyle* analogy kicks back in, because when Jimmy Buffett was just a hustling young musician I have to think it was all pretty generic. Yeah, I know, I'm generalizing here, and possibly overstating. In any case, when Jimmy Buffett was just starting out, it's probably a safe bet to suggest that nobody was very familiar with his music. He was just a guy with a guitar, offering a pleasing mix of soft rock and country to folks who happened to be in the mood for that type of diversion. It was background music, a sweet soundtrack to go with a nice day in the Florida sun or along the streets of New Orleans.

If Amazon could track the listening tastes of Jimmy Buffett's earliest fans, it would be all over the place, because there was nothing to really distinguish this guy's brand of pleasing, soft rock from a couple dozen other folk-singer types with a similar kick-back attitude. He was like a whole bunch of other artists, until he came up with his first hit.

Okay, so that's Jimmy Buffett at the *item* stage of his evolution as a performer. Next, along with his first record deal, he shifted towards *label* status. He had a name and a take-away product listeners could bring home if they wanted to hear more of the same. The big, breakout hits were still to come, but he had an identifiable sound and persona. He went from being *some guy with a guitar* to being *some guy named Jimmy Buffett with a guitar*—and that's a big jump. Folks began to know who he was. Maybe they started to know some of his songs. Still, at this early point in Jimmy Buffett's career, audiences might not have been planning to see one of his shows the way they would later; it might have been more of an impulse thing. Maybe they'd happened by a couple times before or heard one of their buddies say the guy put on a good show, and they figured they'd stop and listen. Most likely, folks were stumbling across him as much as seeking him out, but once they did they knew where to find him if they wanted more of the same later on.

When his songs started to get some air play, and when his concerts started to draw more and more of a following, that's when Jimmy Buffett went from being an *item* to a *brand*. It didn't happen overnight, and you won't be able to find a hard-and-fast line in his album sales or concert grosses—just a steady upward progression until he reached a certain critical mass. Here you can see his album sales start to pick up, and his concert venues get bigger and bigger, his tour dates selling out sooner and sooner, until finally he had his breakthrough hit with Margaritaville. As a successful singer-songwriter *brand*, then, Jimmy Buffett was able to chart a lucrative career path that grew to include albums, t-shirts, concert videos, and every standard tie-in item you might expect to see as an outgrowth of any thriving recording and performing career. It was all connected.

A couple years later, Jimmy Buffett looked up and he had thousands of followers. Hundreds of thousands, probably—maybe more. They called themselves "parrotheads." (Don't even ask me what *that* means.) I was deep into a whole different kind of music scene, so this growing phenomenon was completely lost on me, but these parrotheads flocked to Jimmy Buffett's sold-out shows, which became like mini-vacations for these good people, who found in this guy and his music a way to celebrate the free and easy, escapist mindset even if it was only for a couple hours. And then, when Jimmy Buffett started writing books, they flocked to the bookstores as well. When he opened his first restaurant and bar, they lined up there, too, and here's where the guy morphed into *lifestyle* status. Here's where everything Jimmy Buffett touched had to do with getting drunk and getting chicks and getting the most out of a laid-back attitude that ran completely counter to the corporate grind.

But get this: Jimmy Buffett was Jimmy Buffett long before the public caught on to his message. He was Margaritaville before there was a Margaritaville. The laid-back persona that caught on with millions of fans was Jimmy Buffett's personal brand, first and foremost. It wasn't any kind of manufactured or orchestrated deal. It was genuine. And this right here is the main reason why that message struck such a chord with people, because that's not the kind of persona that can be fabricated or created in a studio. Go that route, and you end up with Vanilla Ice—artists that are "designed" for public consumption, whose careers don't usually last much beyond the one-hit-wonder phase. Same goes for Barack Obama, when he was just getting started in Illinois politics. People responded to him because he was genuine. He wasn't pandering for votes; he was working selflessly and passionately for change. You look at a guys like Barack Obama and Jimmy Buffett and get the feeling they would have been doing the same damn things, in success or failure. Broke or rich, Jimmy Buffett would be singing his songs, living his relaxed, island lifestyle, kicking back. Somehow, he found a way to attach that persona to a money-making brand, but it's a whole lot easier to sell the truth than a fabrication, don't you think? At the end of the day, the easiest thing to sell is the truth.

Like I wrote earlier, I don't listen to Jimmy Buffett's music. It's just not my thing. Chances are, I wouldn't recognize him if I stumbled across him on some island with a couple margaritas in his hands, but I set out his career path here as a winning reminder that sometimes a merchandising push can be so inadvertently and wildly profitable it appears in retrospect to have been carefully conceived all along. And, sometimes, a versatile performer can appear before us fully formed, as if he never went through all these other phases to get where he is today. True overnight sensations are pretty rare in the entertainment business; it might be that a performer rockets to sudden fame on the back of a breakthrough hit or role or appearance, but there's usually a history to it.

Usually, the guy's been at it a good long while.

Winning by Association

The power and significance of branding is so prevalent it reaches all the way across the pop culture spectrum and into "imaginary" brands that first came to public attention in movies and television shows. This has got to be one of the weirdest trends of our information age, but it reinforces the strength and influence of an all-out marketing campaign—*even for products that don't exist*! Duff Beer (the brew of choice from *The Simpsons*) and Nostromo (the spaceship freighter from *Alien*) are just two examples of fake products that have made a real mark with fans. You can actually buy Duff Beer t-shirts and mugs and bottle-openers—all of it promoting a brewery you won't find on any map beyond the animated world of *The Simpsons*. There's even a website for designs and logos relating to some of the most memorable companies in 20ᵗʰ century fiction— www.lastexittonowhere.com—which strikes me as crazy and telling and a fitting reminder of the prominence of a successful brand.

Probably the most current example this *surreality* tie-in branding is a lifestyle beverage called "Tru Blood," which was first featured as a key plot element in the hit HBO teen vampire series *True Blood*. On the show, the vampires drink this stuff for sustenance, from a distinctive bottle—a bottle eerily similar to the one being sold in stores on the back of this licensing deal.

Now, let's bring the discussion back around, because the rules that apply to individuals also apply to corporations. Does your "team" wear your team colors? We know UPS just by the look of those trucks and brown uniforms. Brown has really become a signature color for them. They've even incorporated it into their company tag line: "What can *brown* do for you?" There are other messenger companies out there who might be able to deliver your package in the same way, but the UPS brand has come to own that space for a lot of people. You see their team colors. The brown box, the brown shorts, the brown truck, and on and on. And there's buy-in from the UPS team, too. Everybody's on the same page.

One of the best moves I made in launching FUBU was getting my clothes on the backs of celebrities and rappers. It's not like we had any money to actually *pay* some star for his or her endorsement, but it was no random effort. No, a great deal of thought went in to figuring out if this or that artist reflected our clothing line in the best possible light. Did he represent our core values? Did he appeal to our targeted customer? Did he look *good* in our clothes? And, just as important, did our clothes look like they fit with the artist's style? You have to realize, the wrong celebrity endorsement can kill a brand just as surely as the right celebrity endorsement can send sales through the roof—and here the celebrity endorsements really paid off for us, first with just one or two rappers and eventually a whole mess of rappers and hip-hop artists who spoke to the same audience. The *right* placement of the *right* garment in the *right* music video meant the world to us when we were just starting out.

Once again, timing is everything, right?

Back in the day, of course, music videos were a whole lot more relevant than they are today, and if we tried to launch FUBU in our current digital age we'd have to go about it a different way. We'd have to have our own YouTube channel or MySpace page or Twitter feed, and drive traffic to our sites with short, clever, streetwise videos. We'd have to have our own, revolutionary website, with all kinds of crazy links and exciting graphics and a huge interactive component, and set it up so that it became a real destination site for our customers. But music videos did the job for us back then.

That was the "space" where young people tended to congregate, so we hit them where they lived.

Another key was recognizing at some point early on that our customers were investing in me and my partners every time they put on our clothes. It didn't start out that way, but that's where we ended up. On the way, we ran into a whole bunch of people rooting for us to succeed who were also in a position to help us do so. This, too, is key. A successful start-up needs people to invest in the operation—not just customers, but in our case local promoters, boutique owners, printers, embroiderers, and on and on. One of the best examples of this is Ralph McDaniels, who became a kind of tastemaker to the black community through his influential *Video Music Box* show on public access television. It was like some street version of the *Good Housekeeping* seal of approval. (As long as I'm on it, there's another great brand for you, one that still symbolizes quality and value, long after the magazine that gave it authority lost some of its relevance.) With Ralph, it was more than just a passing endorsement. He took a liking to our clothes and our business plan. He took a liking to the four of us, on a personal level as well. He liked that we were four kids from the streets, looking to build something out of nothing. And so, by talking us up, he *invested* in us. That's the kind of push every business needs just starting out. You need people rooting for you—people in your own communities, with some kind of interest in your success.

(By the way, "Uncle Ralph" is still doing his thing—still relevant, still making a difference. You can check him out at OnFumes, a social networking site that builds on his *Video Music Box* roots and enhances his *brand* as a hip-hop tastemaker on the R&B video scene.)

In our case, Ralph's support led to all kinds of support from local promoters, boutique owners, printers, and embroiderers— all manner of local businessmen and women who stood to gain in some intangible way if our business succeeded. Either they invested in me and my partners the same way Ralph McDaniels invested in us, or maybe they just didn't want to bet against us. Either way, they were with us. It started out that folks just liked the look of our stuff, and the price, but after a while they got hip to the fact that we were just a bunch of guys from the neighborhood, trying to make some noise in the fashion industry, and they responded to that as well. It was a double bonus.

It's the same with other companies, in other industries. When we reach for an iPod or a Mac laptop, we're investing in Steve Jobs, not just in Apple. When we download the latest version of Windows, we're investing in Bill Gates, not just in Microsoft. When we sign on at a new gym or enroll in a martial arts class or start a regimen of dietary supplements, we're investing in Bruce Lee. When we vote the rest of the Democratic ticket on election day, we're investing in Barack Obama. There's such a fine line between the business and the business leader, the movement and the movement leader, that when a guy like Steve Jobs looks sick, giving a speech to shareholders, you can see the stock price of his company start to drop just on speculation over his health, and then spike when he makes his way back.

At some point, the company and the innovators behind it become so intertwined in the public consciousness that there's no telling one from the other—and that's when a brand can really make a full-on leap into becoming a successful lifestyle company. They can own the space they created *and* everything that touches it, even in a peripheral way. At Apple, there was a time when they were just about computers, but now they're all about everything electronic, all these gadgets and gizmos that add to the quality and ease and efficiency of our lives and our enjoyment of popular culture. Would you buy an Apple television at this stage in the company's development? Hell, yeah. Would you buy Apple clothing, if it had one of those trademark apples on it, and a futuristic design, and maybe some pockets that were wired for your iPhone or your iPod? Hell, yeah.

Success in Motion

What about BlackBerry? A lot of people don't know the company behind BlackBerry, Research in Motion (RIM), but the BlackBerry has become so ubiquitous that I can certainly see RIM offering new line of products, building on the BlackBerry image. What does BlackBerry stand for? What are its "team" colors? For my money, it represents the exchange of information. It's all about clarity, precision, speed. Why couldn't they grow into a line of music-related products, or televisions, or home-based information equipment? As long as you stayed true to those core values—clarity, precision, speed—you could find all kinds of different ways to build the brand into a full-fledged lifestyle, focused on the exchange of information. And it appears the people at RIM are aiming to do just that, judging from their latest "Love What You Do" ad campaign, which is more about lifestyle than hardware. As I write this, BlackBerry has control of its market, and it's what they do with that control that will stamp the company going forward.

That's the dilemma we faced at FUBU, after our first taste of success. Once our customers let it be known that they were getting behind me and my partners, we came to realize that our morals, actions, decisions, and foresight would all come back to haunt us or reward us as a brand over time. It was all tied in to our success and our image—and, over time, our integrity became one of FUBU's biggest assets. Even if we decided to suspend production on a line, as we've done over the years, or take a product off the market for a certain period, as we've also done, we knew we could come back to it later as long as we'd established the right level of trust with our customers.

But even though that trust was one of our strengths, it's also where we were vulnerable. Over time, our competitors realized that the only way to fight us was to sling mud. From our big beginning at FUBU, when we started working with Samsung, a move that brought us all-important distribution to fill our first orders while allowing us to keep control of every aspect of the company, folks who wanted to take us down started to suggest we had sold out. We tried to stay out in front on this, and we always talked openly about our partnership arrangement, but the integrity we had built with our "For Us, By Us" message was still thrown into question, and we learned the hard way how difficult it is to scramble back from those kinds of attacks.

Those attacks find you on a personal level, too, and one of the most glaring examples of this is the way some people in the black community came out gunning for Beyonce, shortly after she became a triple threat, in movies, music, and fashion. You can't say anything bad about this girl. She is beautiful. She sings great. She can dance. She can act. She treats her colleagues with respect. So where's that mud gonna come from? It's like she was bullet-proof, but then you started hearing that she had bad breath. It was all over the clubs, spread by people who wanted to cut her down for whatever reason. But you really had to consider the source here. I mean, who was able to get close enough to this singing, dancing, acting *goddess* to even make such a statement with any kind of first-hand authority? I've met her a bunch of times, and believe me, this woman smells sensational—head to toe, I'm sure. And she looks ten times better in person than she does in her videos. But that's how people try to cut you down when your brand is so effective. They look for any way they can to poke holes in what you've built and bring you down to size—but hey, over time, when the dust settles, the rumors go away and you stand on your own. That's how it happened for us at FUBU, and for Beyonce, too.

By the Book

At FUBU, we're not the same company we were when we just started out. No way. If we were, I'd still be selling those shirts and hats from a duffel bag outside Queens Coliseum in Jamaica. We've changed it up, and that's the way it goes with almost every successful lifestyle brand. And, we made our share of mistakes—a whole bunch of them, actually. We even disappeared for a while, pulling our FUBU line out of the American market around 2003, and looked to build things in Europe and Asia. One of the reasons for this was that we had gotten a little too big, too quickly. We over-distributed in the United States. We got so carried away with our early rush of success that we were busting at the seams, racing to get the goods out there, getting ahead of ourselves.

It got to where we had so much excess inventory, we had to put it into discount outlets like Burlington Coat Factory and Filene's just to get back some of our investment. This turned out to be a big mistake, and it could have hurt us long term if we didn't stay on top of it. When you saturate the market like we did, you lose whatever allure or cache you might have had when you first launched. I'm not so sure we recognized this going in, but we figured it out soon enough. In the fashion industry, once you hit those mark-down bins, it's tough to climb your way out of them, because you've lost the sense that your clothes are fresh and vibrant and new. That can be the kiss of death to a clothing line. All of a sudden, there's a low-rent, discount taint to your product, and the customers you sought starting out won't be caught dead in your clothes.

Another mistake we made, early on, was limiting our distribution seasons. In the clothing business, a lot of companies deliver a new line ten times each year—almost every month. At FUBU, we stuck to the seasons and delivered only four times each year—winter, spring, summer, fall—but this ended up hurting us. It meant that if a kid went into a store in January he'd see our winter line, and if he went back to that same store again in March he'd see that same line. Over time, after a couple visits, our clothes would start to appear stale, especially when you put them up against the new product these other manufacturers were putting out there month after month. We should have spread it out, like we do now, so that when a kid goes in there, he sees something new every time.

Also, we fell into the bad habit of prepacking our clothes and forcing retailers to take set shipments of twelve garments, bundled together in sizes of our choosing. Usually, we'd send out two larges, three XLs, three XXs and four XXXs. (Our sizes tended to run big—not because our customers tended to run big, but because none of them wanted to reach for a small or a medium.) The pre-packaging made sense, we thought, because it cut down on our shipping and packaging costs, but it turned out that by forcing these 12-count packages on all retailers we started to see a lot of excess inventory in stores. Maybe the sizes didn't match the needs of their clientele, which of course the merchants would have known better than us, or maybe it was a boutique that just didn't handle the kind of volume we were expecting. Our clothes would start to pile up and we wouldn't ship new goods to these stores until they sold through the old stuff. We found ourselves in a real logjam.

The only way to respond to all these missteps, we thought, was to pull the line for a while, and let demand for FUBU product build itself back up. Or, not. It wasn't until a couple years later, though, that we hit on a way to tap back into the market—through Twitter and Facebook and other social networking sites that had surfaced in the time since we took our product off the shelves. All of a sudden, I was able to gauge what our target customer was thinking when he thought about FUBU—if he even thought about FUBU at all. Remember, these sites didn't even exist when we started out, and they hadn't been any kind of presence when we put things on pause, and then I looked up one day and saw that this essential two-way marketing tool had just fallen into our laps. It was a great gift, really. I'd go on to Twitter and "hash-tag" the word FUBU and pay attention to what came back in response. And as I searched I got to thinking that this was what all CEOs should be doing for their brands, because it's the purest acid test you can have. If I saw 100 FUBU mentions, it might have turned out that 85 percent of them didn't really know what we're about, or that we had essentially been out of the market for a couple years. I now had the ability to fire back and say, "Hey, if you're seeing anything out there with our name on it, it's either six or seven years old or it's counterfeit." Over time, when you start educating people about your product, it builds up a whole new demand for it. And, a whole new sense of loyalty and belonging. I started to hear back from some of these kids I was connecting with online, and they were telling me, "You know what, I'd be ready to see some of that stuff again." Or, some of the old guard would check in and say, "Hey, Daymond, where you been? I'm ready for something new!"

All along, the perception of FUBU was that we were all about baggy jeans and that old hip-hop look, and for a time that was our signature style, but what these people didn't realize was that for the past years we'd been pushing that slender European fit. We may have been one thing here in the States, but now we were something else, overseas. Slowly, that message took hold, the perception changed, and then it built from there. Then we had some older people weigh in and start to educate these younger Twitter followers about our line of clothes and what FUBU had meant to their generation.

Fortunately for us, the FUBU brand has grown to where we can adapt it to almost anything. We've built enough trust and goodwill over the years so that many of our core customers will follow us to all kinds of places. Yeah, we started out selling clothes, but now we can lend that street-smart, self-empowered sensibility to vacation resorts and frozen foods, just to offer up two examples. Think about it. A FUBU beach vacation can be like a hip-hop Club Med, down in the Caribbean, catering to successful young professionals (black and white and every color in the rainbow) and featuring a certain kind of music, a certain kind of food, a certain kind of décor. A FUBU foods line could be smothered pork chops and fried chicken and waffles—the kind of comfort food usually thought of as soul food, dressed up for the frozen foods aisle to satisfy an upscale urban crowd anxious for the tastes of home but accustomed to the convenience of a prepared meal from Stouffer's or Swanson's.

I think back on how we've changed and grown at FUBU and it puts me in mind of one of the great names in retail—Tiffany. A lot of folks don't know this, but Tiffany started out selling pots and pans; the jewelry came later. Listerine began as a floor cleaning product; the personal hygiene and mouthwash stuff came later. (Hey, maybe I can hook them up with Beyonce for a line of commercials with some serious heat—ha ha!)

You start out one thing and end up another. It happens all the time, in every business. You have to be willing to adapt—and this, too, needs to be a part of a company's branding strategy. The key, really, is to build your company on a strong base. It's just like a building. If you build it on a weak foundation, if it's not level, or if it's sinking and there are cracks everywhere, it won't stand for very long. If you get the groundwork just right, you'll be around for a good long while.

It works the same way for you as an individual. Stand on a firm foundation, carry yourself with strength and confidence, and you're the man. Follow the crowd in a tentative, uncertain way, and you'll crash and burn. Align yourself with the right people, forge the right relationships, and you'll set yourself up for the long run.

Another key is recognizing when the time is right to sell, reinvent or discontinue your brand. There's a clear lifecycle to some products and services. You can almost chart it, based on sales, public response, whatever. The visionary business leader will know when that cycle has peaked, and when it might come around again, and respond accordingly, just like a strong individual will be well-positioned to reimagine himself from time to time, to keep ahead of the curve.

Branded!

*"Here's how I think of my money, as
soldiers. I send them out to war every day.
I want them to take prisoners and come home,
so there's more of them."*

—Kevin O'Leary

JUST ONE IDEA
The Thick 'n Sweet Casebook – Vol. II

Last we checked, we had the idea to start pouring maple syrup on some hot, hardly dressed females in a shameless strategy to sell the stuff to hot-blooded American males. A sure-fire concept, right? A why-didn't-I-think-of-that business plan that just pops right out at you, wouldn't you agree?

Well, let's break it down and see what we've got.

The key to any successful new product launch is to start small. Aim too high right out of the gate and you're bound to come up short. Keep it simple and within reach, and at least you'll have some kind of shot. In the music business, this means developing a local following before hitting the road and taking your act on tour. (The thinking here is that if you can't even get the folks in your hometown to check you out, the folks around the country who don't know you at all won't check you out, either.)

In fashion, it means building a real demand for a certain look or style in one particular region, and then filling that demand and building on it before taking it wide. (The thinking here is that if you can't spot the trends well enough to dress the people next door, you'll be flying blind everywhere else.)

It's especially important that you start small in the food business, particularly the novelty food business, where you have to worry about storing and shipping perishable goods, and every mile outside your wheelhouse cuts into your bottom line. So that's where we're at here with our fictional maple syrup business.

Word of mouth is key at the grassroots level, and that's where you want to be when you're just getting things off the ground on a new venture because, chances are, you won't have a budget for a broader, more far-reaching push. Another key is to focus on quality. Our maple syrup business doesn't go anywhere unless the stuff is good—mouth-watering, taste-tempting, recipe-sharing good. The kind of good you want to holla about. This goes without saying, but I'll say it anyway. Doesn't matter what you're peddling, it needs stand a cut above whatever else is out there, otherwise you're just grabbing at an impulse buy, the one-shot money we talked about earlier. Your product needs to be first rate, like this kid in the club suggested. Without the quality, it's just about the packaging; you'll have the introduction, but not the follow through. Yeah, you might get a bunch of folks to give you a shot, and you might make some money early on, but you won't get too many repeat customers if you don't deliver on your promises. Nobody will care about your clever packaging or raunchy promotion. You'll be a short-haul player in a long-haul field.

If you're starting small, it's a good bet you've got a budget to match, so you'll want to get the pieces of your Thick 'n Sweet puzzle together on the cheap. Doesn't mean you have to cut corners, just go about things in a ground-level way. The good news here is that you don't need a bunch of money to start an entry-level marketing campaign for a hard-charging homestyle syrup, especially if you're looking to ramp up in your hometown. That's always my recommendation when someone talks to me about a new product or new business launch. It makes sense to start in a market you know, where folks know you, where you know what's worked in the past, and where whatever angles you'll need to play or holes you'll need to plug will be most readily apparent.

Most of us have heard that old expression used to describe a product or concept that seems like a natural—"It sells itself." Well, there's no such thing as a product or concept that sells itself. It's just a line. Truth is, you've got to help it along, and some ideas need more help than others. This holds true for pretty much any new product you can think up—any new service, or concept, or establishment. You can't count on any kind of viral marketing or word-of-mouth to talk you all the way up and announce your arrival. That stuff helps, and it's important, but you can't count on it. You've got to generate it, and work at it. To start, you'll need a logo that smartly announces your name and the nature of your business, along with a sense of fun and sizzle (or, a sense of seriousness and value, if that's what you're going for), and you can probably design one yourself that will serve you well enough to get started. Or maybe you can hit up a graphic artist neighbor or cousin to help you out.

When you think about it, the only enterprise that doesn't need to market its goods and services is the United States Mint—and they actually do spend a whole lot of time and money on marketing, so there's no avoiding it.

Next, you'll need to hire a model (or three), who'll be willing to let you pour syrup all over them, and pose them in erotic, suggestive ways. Not exactly the most wholesome gig in the history of modeling, but you're bound to find some takers. Remember, this is the core of your marketing strategy, so you don't want to cut corners here, but at the same time you've got to cover your costs. This is one area that could run into some money if you're not careful, so get out in front and look for ways to get your models to pose for free.

(Tip: be sure to have them bring their own bathing suits, because there probably won't be a wardrobe line in your advertising and promotion budget.)

You're looking for that all-important hometown edge, the solid turn that is far more likely to come your way in your own neighborhood, where you're known and where folks are inclined to root for you or do you some type of solid, than you are out there in the great wide open. Hopefully, you'll have a girlfriend or a sister, someone who is relatively hot and a relative good sport, and with any luck she'll have a couple friends who are the same way. They might take the job just for the good time, or for the portfolio of pictures you'll be able to offer them at the other end, or maybe they'll be down for a case of free syrup. Or maybe you'll get lucky and you'll stumble across the flamboyant, extrovert types you'll need to make your pitch, because the assignment doesn't have to end with this one photo shoot. Ideally, you're looking for a long-term relationship.

In success, you'll want to establish a stable of "Thick 'n Sweet" girls you can call on to make promotional appearances at local clubs and stores. (Of course, you could go at this with a bunch of guy models too, but that's a whole other business plan!) Dress your "Thick 'n Sweet" girls in a stylin' uniform of cut-off tee's or halter tops and make them you're syrup ambassadors. You'll want to hire them to hand out t-shirts and ball caps at special events. And, if you're really thinking ahead of the curve, you'll want to make sure there are a couple of video cameras on hand at your photo shoot, so you can document making of 'Thick 'n Sweet' to post on YouTube or MySpace. Or, if you're on a social networking site like Twitter, you can find a way to list all the different locations where folks can find your syrup.

Make it worth your while in what ways you can afford, and see what comes your way. You might not get to work with a *Sports Illustrated* swimsuit model (there's the power of that *SI* brand we talked about earlier!), or a Victoria's Secret lingerie girl (and the power of that one, too!), but with a little scrambling and a little luck you can certainly expect to hustle your way into *Hustler* territory. (Okay, so *Hustler* isn't exactly the prestigous brand association you're shooting for here, but for our purposes it might be just enough to do the job.)

Then, once you've got your "Thick 'n Sweet" girls all lined up, you can call on them to appear alongside a display at your local market, or to accompany you as you visit a neighborhood construction site or college football game to give away some samples, or whatever other strategy you can think up.

The primary tie-in goal here is to produce a simple poster that you can then plaster all over town—in bodegas, barber shops, CD stores, wherever . . . Produce a couple hundred extras, so you can hand them out and hope like crazy some high school kids and local frat boys want to put them up on the walls of their bedrooms. No nudity, and no downright nastiness, because you'll need to slap these posters all over the public place, and in this way build a base-level brand awareness that hopefully sticks. That's a big concept in marketing these days—"sticky branding," they call it. (No, it's not the most academic term, but marketing experts aren't exactly a bookish bunch.) The idea is to create an emotional attachment between your target customer and your product, but like a lot of grand marketing concepts, this can be an elusive goal. The thing is, no one is ever entirely sure how to do this. Really, you never know what sticks. I don't care how many college and post-graduate degrees you've got, all you can do is be creative and out there and hope to catch a break. If these Madison Avenue-types could predict with any kind of certainty that their campaigns would hit their mark every time out, things like marketing and branding and advertising would be more of a science than an art. You give it your best shot. You develop a feel, a gut, a nose for what might work, and then you attach that to what you can afford, put it out there, and hope to see results.

As long as we're in the kitchen on this one, think of it like making spaghetti. When you want to make sure your noodle is good and cooked, you toss it up to the ceiling. If it sticks, it's ready. If it drops to the floor, it's still got some boiling to do. Sticky branding, then, is the art and not-quite science of throwing a bunch of ideas at the ceiling to see what sticks. Toss enough of them, and something's bound to grab hold. Toss just a couple and you might miss out entirely.

One of the great things you've got going for you is that your Thick 'n Sweet campaign is a fun, original, out-there concept. Pouring maple syrup on pretty girls? Connecting something wholesome, like eating pancakes and waffles and French toast, with something scandalous and shocking, like scantily-clad women rolling around in food products? Eating and looking at hot girls in scanty clothes—two all-American pastimes? Who can't get behind that? Whatever photo shoot you're able to arrange, it's bound to be a memorable affair—for the models, the photographer, the set designer, and on down the line. Shouldn't be too much of a problem rounding up talented, enthusiastic friends to help with the logistics, and to help you place your posters and fliers all around town, even if you've got next to nothing to pay these good people. At the very least, your models will get some great shots to add to their portfolios—and your boys will get treated like casting agents for one day. Plus, everyone will get to score some syrup out of the deal, so you can set it up as a win-win all around.

Here again, the local angle is probably going to be one of the principle elements of your launch strategy. After all, where else can you tap into all of this sweat equity, like you'll get from your friends and family? Your boys are way more likely to help you out on something like this than a bunch of perfect strangers just looking to eyeball some syrupy models. Plus, the people in your area would love to be a part of a movement, to feel like they're on the ground floor of the next big thing. I keep coming back to this sense of belonging, I know, but it's an essential element at almost every stage of almost any successful launch. It's not just your customers who want to feel like they're signing on to some happening thing. It's the friends and family you can rope in to help you. It's everyone who will have a hand in getting your business off the ground, the folks who like to feel like they were in on the ground floor, at the very beginning. They'll talk up your product and help spread the word in a much bigger, more meaningful way than if you started someplace other than home, so look first in your own backyard before branching into foreign territory.

From here, you'll spend some time on the manufacturing front—because, of course, it's one thing to have a sweet, quality recipe, and quite another to crank it out in a big-time, noticeable way. You'll have to contact bottlers and distributors and make sure you're ramped up to meet any sudden surge in demand. The packaging should be distinctive, unusual—maybe it should call to mind a bottle of suntan lotion, to reinforce the way you're applying it to all these hot models in your advertising. (Man, these ideas are just too good to give away in a book, don't you think?) Or maybe it should be shaped like a big old mayonnaise jar, with a wide-mouth opening and a big wooden spoon with your logo on it affixed to the package, which could really help you stand apart in the syrup aisle. Do your research. Roam the syrup aisle at the grocery store. See what's out there, and what comes to mind. Maybe you'll come up with some other packaging gimmick, like selling the syrup along with a basting brush, encouraging people to paint the syrup on their pancakes and waffles instead of pouring it on, reinforcing the hot, R-rated images of your primary campaign, and in a not-so-subtle way encouraging your customers to consider these other, more outrageous uses of your product in the privacy of their own homes.

Let your imagination go crazy, because that's where your budget is truly unlimited; it doesn't cost a cent to come up with a great marketing idea—it's the execution of that great marketing idea that might be hard to afford. Thinking on the cheap, then, maybe there's a theme to be mined from the R-ratedness of this whole deal. Maybe one of your tag lines can talk about the Triple R-rating of your product.

(RRR—as in, "Really Sweet, Really Thick and Really Good.")

Or, go all the way with your down 'n dirty campaign and come up with some kind of suggestive, Triple X-rated copy.

(XXX—as in, "Xtra Thick, Xtra Sweet and Xtra Special!)

Maybe you'll want to tinker with the product itself, so that it stands out in ways other than taste and texture, like experimenting with food dyes. (Hey, a red maple syrup! Now we're cooking!) Or maybe you can come up with some way to make a clear-colored syrup, which just might open the door to a whole other marketing campaign as a healthy, lite alternative to the traditional maple blend. As long as the FDA gives you the necessary approval, and all your ingredients check out, what do you care if the syrup looks a little funky?

In the beginning, you'll probably just need a couple dozen cases of maple syrup, which you can place on consignment in specialty stores and restaurants in your area—perhaps a pancake house or diner known for its fresh, family-style food and heaping portions. Or, a local bar and grill that happens to serve breakfast. Approach them the right way, with the right incentives and the right mix of professionalism and enthusiasm, and you should have no trouble finding at least a couple places to carry your syrup on their tables and put it on display by the cash register. You can even reach out to those independent catering-truck operators, who drive to factories and construction sites and sell coffee and pastries and breakfast sandwiches, and see if they'll carry your product.

You might not have the money to design the custom bottles of your dreams when you're just starting out, but you're only talking about a couple dozen cases here. You can certainly scrape up some interesting jars or old beer bottles from a generic source and use these for the time being, along with an attractive custom label that picks up on some of the design elements from your poster or other signs.

The idea is to do the best you can with what you've got—and hope it catches on.

Branded!

*"Any damn fool can put on a deal,
but it takes genius, faith and
perseverance to create a brand."*

—David Ogilvy

FOUR

Hustle

Where I grew up, when I grew up, we all had a love for the same nice things. Cars, jewelry, clothes, a nice place to live. We were like any other group of kids, from any other neighborhood. We wanted what we couldn't have so easily, what was just out of reach. We wanted every symbol of success and style we could get our hands on—and a few more besides.

To get these nice things, most of my friends started looking for ways to make money illegally—jacking cars, selling drugs, hitting convenience stores, whatever. Didn't matter to them that it was against the law. Didn't matter what their mothers or their little brothers might think if they could see what they were doing. Didn't even matter that they could get caught or killed. It only mattered that they could get away with it, and make some money on the back of it. And guess what? From time to time, they did just that. More often than not, in fact. Sure, a bunch of guys I used to run with ended up in jail. Yeah, more than a couple of them are dead and gone. And a couple more just fell off everyone's radars and no one ever knew what happened to them.

But truth be told, a lot of these hustles paid off for a lot of my boys, and these pay-offs kept them going until the next hustle, and the one after that—until finally, eventually, inevitably, they didn't.

(Guess you can only skate on thin ice for so long before the ice gives way, huh?) I actually did an inventory at one time in my life, running through my friends and acquaintances to see who was dead, jailed, or successful. It was like a weird little street-corner game I played in my head, but underneath it was a hard-earned truth. Then I'd count up the number of drug-dealers I happened to know, even the low-level guys, and try to figure out which ones were still on the street, making money. I tried to weigh their probable earnings against what they probably had to pay out over the years for lawyers to get their asses out of trouble, what they had to pay in child support and restitution and every other way of making good on their bad turns, and how much they probably lost when they were stuck in jail. When I looked at it this way, amortized over time and circumstance, I realized these guys were making no more than minimum wage—and in some cases, they were making a lot less. The money might seem big for a while, but that while never lasted too long. Plus, there was all that aggravation and worry and hassle.

Didn't seem worth it.

Cover Your Tracks

Forget about doing the right thing. That's a whole other argument. For me, just then, it was about doing time. And coming out ahead. I'm not proud of myself or the kid I was back then, but all I cared about was getting mine and not getting caught. This last part was not because I was too terribly worried about getting in trouble, or catching heat from my mother, but because I hated the idea of being taken out of circulation. Sidelined. Shelved. Set aside in any way. You see, where I came from, with the guys I ran with, time was money. Take yourself out of circulation for any stretch of time, and you'd miss out on a whole lot of paper. Add on all these lawyer bills and other related expenses that tended to come up when you had to clean up your legal messes, and you were way behind guys like me who were choosing to follow the right road. It was like the street version of the tortoise and the hare story. Slow and steady wins the race, right? I don't care what kind of ridiculous success you might enjoy for a year or two. I don't care if you're rolling in money. Spend five years in jail and then tell me it was worth the trade. And this particular counterargument only applied if you happened to make it off the streets alive, because one guy in five would be dead long before the cops caught up to him.

That road wasn't for me. Yeah, I wanted those same nice things. Yeah, I believed, same as everyone else, that these things help to lift me as a brand above those people in my community who were fighting for attention—basically, to get women. That was the end game back then, same as it is now. But slow and steady gets the girl, too. Slow and steady can keep you on that right road, and that right road can still take you where you want to be. Only thing is, it might take you a little while longer to get there.

See, when I looked at myself in the mirror, I knew I wasn't tough enough or stupid enough or heartless enough to go out and hurt someone just to get what I wanted. It wasn't in me to steal. It wasn't in me to put myself at risk or jeopardize my freedom. It wasn't in me to trade right for wrong. All around me, people were taking shortcuts, chasing down their own dreams, but at the same time every other person I knew was either dead or in jail or headed towards one or the other. No, they didn't get caught every time out, but they all got caught eventually. I didn't want that, so I had to find some way to pay for the things I wanted and still be hot and not put myself at risk.

So what did I do? I started a van business. I took a job at Red Lobster. I worked until I dropped. Minimum wages. Tips. Some big pay-off, every here and there. I always had two jobs going, sometimes three. And on the side, there was always some other hustle—a legitimate hustle, but a hustle just the same. This was the beginning of me trying to define my own personal brand. All around, there were kids trying to be one thing or another. They were on their way to setting themselves up on the same *item, label, brand, lifestyle* track I talked about earlier. The get-rich-quick-or-die-tryin' crowd? They were on their way to jail, or to the mall, knee-deep in dealing drugs and stealing cars and running all kinds of illegal hustles. The kids in music class? They were on their way to making some serious noise on the hip-hop scene. The kids on the debating team would soon be our power attorneys, while the kids in art and dance class were laying the foundation for careers as music video directors or choreographers. It was all connected, and the connections started early.

Me, I went to school, I did my thing, and then after hours I punched the clock and went to work on my legitimate hustles. My friends were making easy money, but at least I stood my ground with them. Over time, they came to know me as a person of principle. I didn't start out that way, but that's how I ended up. In the beginning, it was mostly me not wanting to get shot or locked up. In the end, it was me wanting to do the right thing. However it came about, whatever it meant, the Daymond John brand came to stand for something. It stood for keeping out of trouble and sticking to your beliefs and working hard and smart to meet your goals, and I think my friends understood and respected that. It got to where it attracted other people like me. We sought each other out. Not on purpose, mind you, but we tended to gravitate towards each other. You know, like the saying goes, "Birds of a feather flock together."

In my case, growing up, that was really true. I had my hard-core group of friends, and then I started to build another group of friends. Typically, you can tell a lot about a person by the people they choose to deal with, only in my case I was so all over the place it was tough to get a good read on who I was or what I wanted to accomplish. I was keeping my options open, I guess, and setting things up in all these different ways, never quite knowing which path might open up for me—and this, too, became a kind of signature aspect of character for me. I was into everyone and everything, in such a way that I would not let myself be tied-down or pigeon-holed as any one thing.

Not yet, anyway.

Doing My Own Thing

I realize now that even my hardcore friends had their principles. Even a crackhead has a principle. It just wasn't a principle I happened to share, that's all. They all stood for something, too. It just wasn't what I wanted to stand for, that's all. We were different, that's all. I still hung out with these down-and-dirty types, though. Wasn't willing to give that up. Hey, they were my boys! Just because I was slow and steady didn't mean I couldn't hang with the fast and furious. The way it worked was we'd be out, doing our thing, and whenever it was time for their grimy business to go down, they'd just drop me off. They'd be like, "Daymond's in the car, let's pull over." Three or four times a week, this would happen. Check that: for these guys, it was pretty much an everyday thing. For me, I only signed on when I wasn't working, or when I didn't have someplace else I needed to be. We'd hang out at the pool hall off the corner of Farmers Boulevard and Mangin Avenue every day after school. Or maybe we'd hit the corner store, play a little football in the street, talk to some girls, head uptown. Every day it was something different—but then, every day it was also pretty much the same, if you know what I mean. Just chillin', doing our thing, making some noise. Around seven, eight, nine o'clock at night, some guys would go back to their houses to eat dinner. Some guys didn't have a place to go, so they'd just keep hanging out. And then, after dinner, everybody came back. That's how it went.

Eventually, they got down to business. My boys would have to go to work. That's how they looked at it. This was them, punching their own clock. They'd get their guns ready. They'd get their jimmies, to jimmy the car locks. I wouldn't ride with them when they were dirty, just when they were checking things out, scoping out the neighborhood. But once they got their gloves on, and their hammers ready, and whatever else they needed to do their thing, I was gone. See, I was principled, but I was also cool. This was how I justified things in my head, back then. These were my boys. I'd ride with them until I couldn't ride with them and still be true to myself. This was how we spent our time.

Some nights, we'd hit the White Castle first, so the guys who didn't make it home for dinner could get something to eat, and on the way they'd go looking for cars. For a while in there, they were looking for Alfa Romeos, Sterlings, Jettas, and what the 'hood called Baby Benzes (190s). They had a whole ring going on with these cars, stripping them, selling them for parts. They'd spot the cars they wanted, then head back and drop me off, and then pick up another couple guys they needed to help them take the cars. It got to be such a thing between us that I didn't even have to ask to be dropped off.

They just knew.

Now, was it hypocritical of me, to ride along with them, knowing full well what they were doing, and just hop out of the car at the last possible minute and think I was coming away clean? Maybe, but I don't see it that way. The way I see it is that I wasn't some hall monitor. It wasn't my job to snitch on my crew. I'd known these cats since grade school. We were childhood friends. We'd be friends our whole lives—or, at least, until one by one they were killed or thrown in jail or sent packing. It didn't make sense for me to cheat myself out of my time with my crew, so that's how I weighed it in my head. You have to realize, I was an only child. These were my brothers. They were the only family I knew. If I got into any kind of trouble on the street, my boys would be there for me, same way I'd be there for them if they needed me. Sometimes I wouldn't even tell my guys about some small beef I had, but then they'd find out about it on their own and go after the guys I had beef with. Guess you could say they had my back. That's how it goes in the 'hood, when you're runnin' with the right crew.

Anyway, we'd hang until whatever was going down had up and gone down—and then, after that, maybe we'd hang some more. Plus, some nights we wouldn't find any cars, because it's not like there was an Alfa or a Sterling on every street corner. So we'd just cruise the neighborhood and whoop it up and do our thing. We were up to no good, I guess, but it was a smaller, more manageable kind of *no good*. It was the kind of *no good* I could justify.

Another thing you have to realize, this was all we knew. It's not like we were hanging out with all these young financial types or these future captains of industry. We weren't going to prep school or college. We went to church, some of us, but we weren't exactly altar boys. Our fathers weren't doctors or lawyers or investment bankers or real estate developers. We were hustlers, man. We went with what we knew, and what we knew were rappers and drug dealers and car jackers. That was our world.

I went back and forth like that for a while, between my old hardcore friends, and the new friends I was making, the ones who were more like me. Striving. Independent. Purposeful. I wouldn't give up one group for the other, but it was somewhere in that righteous middle that I found out who I really was, what I really stood for.

In the balance, after a whole mess of missteps and miscalculations, I found my own brand.

Branding Your Personality, Personalizing Your Brand

Okay, so that's how things happened for me as a kid, developing my own persona and working it to my advantage, but you can find some of the same growing pains in place in most businesses. From the biggest corporations on down to the smallest mom 'n pops, companies go through their own versions of these stops and starts on their way to becoming an ongoing establishment. Sometimes managers are fully aware of this evolution as it takes shape; other times, they figure it out as they go along; or, they don't and things either work out to the good or fall apart over time.

I didn't really take a look at the typical progression of a typical business until we'd launched FUBU in our atypical fashion, but

I've spent some time on this in recent years, as we've attempted to grow our brand beyond our initial vision and to jump-start new lines or acquire other companies as part of our overall expansion plans. I look at the "personality" of all these different businesses and it's like a fascinating puzzle, but I had no head for this kind of thinking when we were getting off the ground. That is, until I realized I couldn't ignore it going forward. We'd just happened to hit it right the first time, because my partners and I all seemed to land on the same page, with a concept and a line of clothes that seemed to hit the right notes with the right group.

We had our failures—some big, some small—but I knew full well that if I wanted to build on that first rush of success I'd have to figure out a few things. Somewhere in there, I came across a progression chart put together by a leading branding consultant named Jonathan Paisner, who does his thing for a think-tank company called CoreBrand Communications. I met Jon when I was working with his brother Dan on my first book, "Display of Power," and he turned me on to some of the work he was doing on the growth and evolution of corporations over time. Basically, it's the stuff we did by sense and feel the first time around, but I wanted to know why that FUBU launch worked as well as it did; I wanted to slap a name on the things we hit right, so we could repeat those successes on some other venture.

What I learned, reading over Jon's shoulder, is that successful companies go through external *and* internal progressions, and that both sides need to come together in a seamless way if you want your the business to survive and thrive in a competitive marketplace. Makes sense, right? I mean, you're not about to have your left hand working in one direction while your right hand works in another. You'll figure out a way for the two sides to work together, in sync, maybe even help each other out.

Say you've got a start-up underway. Right out of the gate, you'll want to see where you stand relative to where you want to be once you're up and running. On the one side, you'll have all of your external markers in play and a series of related questions you'll need to consider before your launch. On the other side, you'll have the internal factors that'll be more in your control.

Break it down:

- First, you'll have to weigh public awareness of your name and your brand: *Who knows us and what do they know about us?* The idea here is to figure what kind of noise you'll need to make to attract the attention you'll need to succeed, and what kind of noise you might have already made without really realizing it.

- Next, you'll have to quantify the weight of the product or service you hope to offer: *Do we have the expertise to back up our claims?* Basically, this is where you'll decide what space you'll be competing in. You can go high end, or low, or mid market, but you'll have to take a realistic measure before you can expect anyone else to sign on. Don't fool yourself into believing your product is something it's not. And don't go fooling the American public either, because they'll see right through you.

- At some point, you'll have to assess your company's

credibility as well: *Where do we fit among our competitors?* It's one thing to reach for the top shelf in your field, but you'll need to have the goods to back that up. The worst approach you can take starting out is to position your company as a kind of Rolls Royce in your industry, and then start cranking out a Hyundai line. Be consistent.

• And finally, you'll need to figure out the public's confidence in your business and your reputation going forward: *Will our customers feel secure in their decision to work with us?* Basically, the market needs to figure out if you can be trusted. As a kid in Hollis, I was all about the reputation. My rep was my brand, like hard currency, like a "hash-tag" on Twitter, and I could trade on it or build on it or flush it down the toilet. Plug in integrity, loyalty, determination, and all those good things, and what you'd get back was me. The same goes for your reputation in business. When you're in start-up mode, it's the first line in your asset column, but you can't just will it there. You've got to earn it. And, you've got to *keep* earning it, and justifying it, at every turn.

FUBU was an unusual story. We didn't get going in any kind of customary way, but somehow we went on this huge momentum run. We hit it right. If we'd been more like a typical business, I don't think we would have made the same kind of positive, personal connection with our customers, because we were all about keeping it real. They would have seen right through us if we'd gone out and hired all these big-time consultants and market analysts. But that was just us and what we happened to be selling. It wasn't just about the clothes, for us. It wasn't even *mostly* about the clothes, I don't think. Mostly, what we were selling was a sense of belonging, a movement. That's what people responded to. Yeah, the clothes were key, but they were just part of something bigger. *For Us, By Us* . . . it was right there in our name, and when you put on one of our shirts it was right there on your back, too.

Fact is, most big-time companies will need to go through some version of this assessment and analysis phase at some point early in their development, but Jon's twist at CoreBrand is to get entrepreneurs to think internally at the same time they're developing that all-important public image. That's key. To help companies accomplish this, he's come up with a whole other list of measures for management to address from within their own ranks.

Back at it:

- Measure the loyalty of your employees: *Am I proud of my work and my place of work?* Another first and foremost deal. I mean, if your own people can't get behind what you're doing or making or selling, how can you expect any kind of buy-in from the general public? Up and down your corporate ladder, your staff needs to share your passion for your company. They need to *get* it. And, just as important, they need to *get* each other, take pride in each other, root for each other. At FUBU, this might have meant wearing our clothes at work or out in the clubs, or bringing some hot new trend back into our work-space and giving it our own spin.

- Make sure your efforts are aligned with your vision: *Does my work help us meet our goals?* You can't expect someone to work at a task without being able to see the real and tangible relationship between what he or she is doing and your finished product. If your people don't feel like they're making an important contribution, then they're not making an important contribution. Plain and simple.

- Recognize that your hoped-for alignment will need to extend throughout your operation: *Is there a consistent culture and message within the company?* This is something you can tend and nurture in a top-down way. Here's one example: at Ben & Jerry's, the Vermont-based ice cream makers, the business runs on an eco-friendly engine, with the notion that a certain percentage of the profits will go towards making the world a better place. This started with Ben and Jerry themselves, back when they were running the place, and it continues with the current management team and reaches all the way to the guys on the assembly line and in the delivery trucks. Employees are encouraged (and paid!) to volunteer their time to local and national charities, and the caring and compassion comes across in the company's marketing and branding efforts. (And, some people say you can taste all that wholesome goodness in the ice cream!)

- Ensure that your workers have a thorough knowledge of your core business and its underlying values: *Who are we and what do we do?* These days,
more and more companies are standing behind
carefully crafted mission statements, or putting
new hires through an extensive orientation process
to help familiarize them with corporate goals and
histories. If you're in the service industry, say, and
you've built your brand on your white-glove treat-
ment, you'll want to make sure your people on the
frontlines get what you're trying to do.

It's basic, don't you think? But you'd be surprised how many
businesses get going without this kind of guidance or vision. They
go at it in a seat-of-the-pants way, like we did at FUBU, and hope
for the best. But you can't build a business on hope and expect it to
take you anywhere.

Figure it out going in, and figure it out going forward, and
you'll put yourself in a better position to accomplish your goals.

The job of improving your brand is a job that ends the day you go to the pearly gates. Here is a rare picture of me smiling. People feel I'm unapproachable because I rarely smile. How many people have not spoken to me or feared talking to me because the Brand effect they got from me was that I was a mean or stand-offish person? I am constantly working to improve this aspect of my brand. Nothing warms up a room like a smile every once in a while.

It was an honor to be inducted into the National Great Blacks In Wax Museum but it was surely strange looking at ourselves dead in the face as wax figures. Our brand will not only live on by name but as sculptures as well. You can visit the museum at 1603 E North Ave, Baltimore, Maryland 21213.

Keith and I jumped in the picture just to have a little fun with some of our models. Building a personal or public brand is not something you can do yourself. You will always need others who are willing to work with you and help wave the flag. This especially rings true in fashion. Models are a key part of our business.

Although it may look like its a big party but it's a lot of hard work. The men and women we pick to wear our brands must make our product look incredible. I don't think these bikinis would sell if Keith and I were modeling them. Trust me!

As I said, you're a Brand from birth! Just like I am today, I was as a child: strong stance, arms behind my back, chest forward, determined, focused look on my face, no fear of looking you in the eyes. And of course, it was always about fashion. FEAST YOUR EYES ON THAT BOW-TIE, BABY!!!!

One of my biggest regrets is when I turned down a trip to go open our store in South Africa due to other work obligations. Little did I know that Nelson Mandela would hear the FUBU guys were in the country and personally request them to come to his home. On the flip side, one of the greatest moments of my life was to find out that Nelson Mandela knew who we were and my partners actually got to meet him. In my own way, I feel like I was there. I will still meet this mountain of a man.

The top pic is of my partner J and me after a hard day's work sewing hats back in 1992. If you had told us that a clothing line that we would create in the basement of my home would be displayed in the windows of the most famous store in the world, Macy's on 34th Street, I would have told you, "No Way"! If you would have then told me that we would have free-standing stores all around the world, like our store in Milan, Italy, I would have told you that you were crazy and the cheese had definitely fallen off your crackers!!! But think about it. All ideas start somewhere; not it's the opposite with me. When people tell me that something they are working on will never be as big as something else, then I tell them that they are crazy! Your brand and what you do can be as big as you want it, as long as you have the vision.

When I first met Obama in a crowded room of 200 people, he said at the top of his voice, "One of the greatest entrepreneurs of our time." I looked around in shock, wondering who he was talking about. To my surprise, he meant me. Who would ever think the most powerful man in the free world would know of you and your brand?! That is the Brand Power of Barrack: he makes all feel important, and you never forget him once you have watched him on television, heard him on the radio, or had the pleasure of meeting him. I guess that's the reason he is the President.

Here is a picture of one of the gates I personally painted around the city. I painted this gate 12 years ago and it still stands. As I look at it now, it's counter-branding to allow it to remain up this long in this condition. Time to go in the garage; get a couple of cans of paint and white-wash this gate.

I've always said to myself, those guys that open and close the NASDAQ are always waving their hands looking like idiots! So I tried to play it cool in ringing the bell. But the dramatic music, the mood setting lights, and the large screens in the room get you so energized that you can't wait to be one of those idiots waving your hands and smiling. I'm so glad I was able to be part of the Shark Tank ringing the NASDAQ bell.

*On the Shark Tank set, work never stops. The audience only gets
to see 5 minutes of a pitch, but many pitches take an hour or more!
In between them, it's Blackberry time.*

Yes, this is my big head 40 feet long in Times Square! Scary, huh? It was truly an honor to ring the closing bell at the NASDAQ on January 10, 2010. I used to break dance 25 years ago on that same corner for quarters. Now I'm on that very same corner pushing the button that controls 40 billion dollars worth of trading daily.

Branded!

"A brand is a living entity – and it is enriched or undermined cumulatively over time, the product of a thousand small gestures."

—Michael Eisner

FIVE
Long Story Short

FUBU didn't just happen. Oh, we made a big splash, and a lot of people got soaked through by the ripples we made, but it was a long climb to the top of the diving board.

Okay, enough with the "big splash" swimming metaphors. Point is, I've told the FUBU story before, including a pretty thorough account in my first book, *Display of Power: How FUBU Changed a World of Fashion, Branding, and Lifestyle*, but it pays to hurry over some of these same points in these pages, so here goes.

I guess you can say it happened for us pretty much the same way it happens for every successful designer company. Every successful *company*, really. We went through our own version of the *item-label-brand-lifestyle* growing pains, only in our case we didn't always recognize where we fit in the cycle. In fact, I couldn't have put a name or a strategy to the way we went about it if you had put a gun to my head. (Come to think of it, someone *did* put a gun to my head, but that's a whole other story.) We didn't know when we left one stage in our development and entered another; we just knew to keep moving, keep growing, keep changing it up and trying something new. That was our big thing, to keep agile, to find a way to deal with whatever came up. If you want to know the truth, it never even occurred to us to track our growth in any kind of textbook way, or that there was even a cycle to consider. There was no chart or progression we meant to follow. We just kept hustling and climbing, and hustling and climbing, until one day we looked down and we were up pretty high.

I think back on the Michael Eisner quote that precedes this chapter. "A thousand small gestures . . . " That was basically how we pecked away at it, one little thing at a time, only we never saw any one of these early moves as small or insignificant. Plus, the small things have a way of becoming big things. They add up and start to matter. I once worked with a guy who said you can sit on top of a mountain all day long, but you can't sit on top of a needle, and I had no idea what he meant. Still don't. But I liked the image, and it feels to me like it fits right here.

Anyway, that's the picture I have of me and my boys when we were just starting out, getting our thing going at FUBU. We were sitting on top of a needle, balancing all these little things, thousands and thousands of little things, and feeling like we were on top of the world.

Style Points

I never went to college. Never got close to business school, unless I passed some business school building on my way to someplace else. Even high school was a burden—not because I couldn't do the work, but because I couldn't see the need. Wasn't anything those people could teach me that I couldn't learn myself. That was my attitude. I guess I had what people call *street smarts*, but it went beyond the street. It was *instinct smarts*, *market smarts*, *style smarts*. It was all of that, mixed together with a strong survival or preservation instinct. And, to top it all off, it was common sense—and last I checked, they don't teach that in any classroom, and (surprise, surprise) it's not that common, either. You either got it, or you don't, and I thought I had it. I was trying to get and keep some kind of edge over the other guy, no matter what.

I ended up with three partners—J. Alexander Martin, Carl Brown and Keith Perrin—and none of us had a business school background. We each had our own thing, and we came together on the back of our shared dream of making big money. My idea was to get rich before I hit twenty. My idea of rich was a million dollars. That was the finish line for me. Get there, and I'd be set. Get there soon, and I'd be set that much sooner.

My boys felt the same way, and together we set off on our own hip-hop version of the classic rags-to-riches story—never really thinking we had come from *rags*, but at the same time never in our wildest imaginings thinking we'd be rich. We were just off on our next hustle, hoping to make some money until the next idea came along.

It was almost inevitable that our breakthrough came in our own little corner of the fashion industry. After all, it's what we knew. Like a lot of kids in my neighborhood in Queens, I cared about how I looked. My partners were the same way. These days, you'd slap a label on kids who pay such careful attention to their appearance. You'd call them *metrosexuals*, and there'd be a negative taint to it, but nobody had a name for us back then. We were just a bunch of guys, wanting to look good, like everybody else. Yeah, that was our thing, but it was the way of the neighborhood. Hand-in-hand with looking good, we wanted to feel good, and be a part of a movement. I don't think we recognized any of this at the time, but somewhere behind our impulse to dress a certain way, to wear a certain brand, was the desire to feel a part of something. It's the very impulse we ended up building our business on, only back then it was just about dressing alike and fitting in however we could.

I didn't have a whole lot of money, but somehow I managed to put together a closet full of sneakers—and I kept them clean. Out-of-the-box clean. Stand-up-and-notice clean. If I got a smudge or a scuff or any blemish on my kicks, I wouldn't rock them anymore. Sometimes I'd spend a whole Friday night at home, listening to music, cleaning my sneakers with a toothbrush. That's how important it was to me to walk around in clean kicks, and it didn't feel like any kind of chore or ordeal. I was just taking care of my stuff, that's all. To me, there was nothing worse than a pair of grimy sneakers to announce your sorry appearance.

In my neighborhood, if you cared about how you looked, it usually started with your kicks. You worked your way up from there. You messed with the laces in such a way that you developed your own style. Whatever you could do to dress them up, and then you'd try to match them to whatever else you were wearing. If you were creative, if you had a talent for this type of design, it set you apart. You could do anything, really. Whatever little bit of money I did have, I spent it on my feet. Sneakers, mostly, but over time I started buying Timberlands, a couple of pairs at a time. I wore them until they got good and dirty. After that, when they were beyond cleaning, they went to the back of the closet to make room for a new pair—a pair I couldn't really afford but in my head I'd decided I couldn't do without.

The rest of my wardrobe wasn't much, but it was clean and styling. Best I could, I made sure my clothes matched my kicks. That was my thing, my trademark. The color of my shirt had to pick up a color in my sneaker. Maybe I'd wear a hat to pick up the same color, too. My mother made a lot of my clothes, because that was all we could afford. At least, that's how it was until I was about 11 or 12. After that, I started buying my own clothes—with money I'd earn in any number of legitimate jobs and not-so-legitimate hustles. I was always working some angle, always had some deal going. My mother was great on the sewing machine, but at some point I decided I wanted to wear what the other kids were wearing. Meanwhile, she taught me a thing or two about sewing. And about making the best out of a not-so-great situation. She taught me that there was no shame in going homemade, as long as it was homemade with care. At some point, I started putting the same kind of care into the thing or two she taught me about sewing, and eventually *that* became another hustle.

First things first, though: I was always looking at new ways to pick up some paper, and when my boys and I started hanging out at clubs, parties, and concerts I started to pay attention to what the other kids were wearing, what the other kids were buying. At the same time, the other kids were paying attention to what me and my boys were wearing—especially when we hit the road and started going out of town to some of these hip-hop shows and festivals. Back in New York, we were a couple months ahead of the rest of the country, at least in terms of fashion trends, so I started buying up whole bunch of stuff on Delancey Street and carting it down to Philadelphia, Baltimore, DC . . . wherever I happened to be going that weekend. I'd buy name-brand stuff like Osh Kosh, Carhart, Levis, and I'd also buy blanks if that was what I could afford. Goose bomber jackets were big for a while. I'd get some of the stuff tailored, put my own special flair on it, then I'd load up my van and drive to the shows and start selling.

I'd double my money, without a whole lot of effort or risk.

After a couple successful clothing runs, I started branching out into other items I thought I could sell to a concert crowd. Remember those giant Super Soaker water guns? They were pretty popular, and I brought a bunch of them to a couple shows, and they sold like crazy—again, for just about double my investment. Whatever was new or hot or "in," I brought it along and tried to make some paper with it.

One time, on a whim and a loose business plan, I scraped together enough money to buy a bunch of t-shirt blanks, and then I printed slogans on them, like "Free Rodney King!" Slapped a picture of old Rodney on there, too. I did a lot of silk-screening for a while, but this Rodney King episode is one I remember. It was the early 1990s, just after the riots in Los Angeles, and I figured I could haul a couple duffel bags filled with these t-shirts down to a march in Washington, DC, and sell them for a nice profit. I'd had those successful runs, selling my Delancey Street clothes from the back of my van, and lately a lot of my friends had been selling unlicensed shirts at concerts and sporting events. It seemed like easy money, so I went for it. I sold through my inventory in just a few hours, and I remember thinking, *Damn, D, if you just had a little more money to invest you could have sold another couple duffels worth.*

That was my first big-time lesson in business: never underestimate your share of the market, because you'll be caught short. For the most part, opportunity doesn't come banging down your door a second time, so you better be around to answer the call on the first visit. That said, you don't want to bet the farm. That's one of the keys to a successful retail operation, to keep your inventory just right, because once you start overestimating (or, underestimating) you get yourself into trouble. My thing is, if you've got to miscalculate, you're better off keeping too little in inventory, because then you're not left holding the goods. Also, you can create some kind of demand for your product, maybe even increase your price. That's why, when you go to some of these high-end department stores, you might only see one or two pieces of the same design on the rack. It helps to create the impression of demand. Also, if you've got a rack full of the same design, it leaves people thinking there's something wrong with the piece, or it puts it out there that everybody might soon be wearing the same item. You've got to find the right balance.

Branding 101

It never occurred to me to put my name or any kind of label on these shirts. It never occurred to me that I probably should have cut Rodney King in on the profits, so in this one respect at least, it would have been a dumb move to "sign" my shirts in such a way that they could have been traced back to me. I was an idiot, I guess; that's the only way I can explain myself. In any case, I wasn't thinking like a businessman in those days, and I certainly wasn't thinking like a lawyer or some MBA. I wasn't thinking long term. There was no strategy, just hustle. I just wanted to sell through my t-shirts, at $10 each, and call it a good day. And I'd have a bunch more just like it. Each time out, I'd figure some new way to maximize the return on my investment. Maybe I'd dig a little deeper and buy more t-shirt blanks. Maybe the bigger volume would give me enough pull with the wholesaler to get a better price on the blanks. Maybe I'd amp up the sale price—from $10 to $15, say—if I thought the market could absorb the hit.

But this wasn't FUBU. Not yet. This was just a taste. This was just me, figuring things out as I went along, roping in one or two of my boys to help out when I needed an extra pair of hands or another set of wheels. FUBU followed close behind, and here's where my mother's sewing techniques started to pay off. I started making my own line of tie-top hats. Actually, to call it a line at first is to exaggerate. It was a bunch of hats,—just one, to start. I'd seen a particular hat I liked, and looked all over New York to find one, and when I finally hunted one down and checked out the stitching, I decided I could make one myself and do a better job of it besides. I made a couple more for my friends, and after that for friends of friends. People seemed to like them, so I started selling them. I got a few of my boys to help me out. The hats were easy enough to make. Two finished squares of fabric, sewn together to make a hat, with a tie on top for good measure. Each one took about ten minutes to cut and sew, and each one cost me less than a dollar in material. Most of the production fell to me, because I was the only one who could work his way around a sewing table. The more hats I made, they less time they took, and the less they cost. I started out selling them for twenty dollars, and it was almost a straight profit. I didn't count my time back then, because my time was my principal asset and even with all of my other jobs there was plenty of it to go around. I figured I could always rest when I was dead.

Here I'd finally stumbled across the realization that brand identity might play a part in my future in fashion. Of course, I didn't know to call it *brand identity* just yet, but I knew that if people couldn't describe or identify what I was selling they'd never find me, even if I was just hawking my stuff from a duffel bag on the street outside the Coliseum Mall, at 165th Street and 89th Avenue in

Jamaica. And, once they found me and decided they liked the product and the workmanship, they'd never go looking for me again unless my hats had some sort of name.

This was around the time I came up with the name my clothes still carry—only, I kind of backed into it. At first, I thought to call my company BUFU—as in, *By Us, For Us*. Same idea as the *For Us, By Us* notion that would become FUBU, only backwards. My thinking was, since we were selling this stuff on the street, in a homemade sort of way, it made sense to do it under a label that reinforced our small-time roots. It was a way to play on people's desire to do business within their own community. It didn't have to be about black or white, rich or poor. It was feeling a sense of pride or ownership with whatever group or movement you wanted to associate. I wasn't thinking along any *culture, movement, lifestyle* lines in those days, at least not in any kind of full-on, fully-realized way, but that's really what the name was all about. Even if I couldn't articulate it just this way, just yet, it would be a way to connect our customers to us, and to each other. Also, it would be a pride thing, I thought. A way to keep it real, to offer a sense of belonging along with the clothes. This part turned out to be a real key for us, because there was a lot of talk in the neighborhood at the time over a comment made by some executive at Timberland, who'd said his clothes weren't meant for drug dealers. There was this huge rumble in our community when that hit the news. It's like we couldn't believe this guy was stupid enough to say what he'd just said. He used the phrase *urban market* to describe his undesirable customers, but we knew what he meant. Everybody knew what he meant.

The *urban market* was a marketing euphemism for us inner city kids—low-income blacks, whites, and Hispanics who lived in what less-enlightened marketing types might have called the ghetto. It was a huge slap to a lot of us in the neighborhood who had been buying up Timberland boots and outdoor gear by the truckload. The message we took in was that the company didn't want all this attention from rap and hip-hop artists, who had been mentioning Timberland in their songs and wearing the stuff in their concerts and videos, and of course there was a huge backlash—and an immediate drop-off in Timberland sales. With a name like BUFU, we thought, we could speak to all those kids who felt cut off by the Timberland executives, as well as everybody else. We could send a powerful signal that we didn't need their clothes, because we had our own.

Be Prepared to Change It Up

We kicked the name around for a couple days to get a feel for it. To be honest, I think I was probably drunk when I came up with it, and everyone else was probably drunk when they said it sounded pretty good to them, so we needed a little perspective. I came up with it one night at the house, after a hard day of work and a hard night of drinking, but in the sober light of day it didn't seem half-bad. It grew on us. I particularly liked that it was an acronym you could speak out loud. I thought that was cool—and, key. In fact, I liked it so much I started to put it on labels and sew it into the hats. But then someone walked up to me on the street one afternoon and pointed out to me that the acronym I'd been thinking was so great—BUFU—could also be read a different way. The guy spoke with a thick Southern accent. He said, "You gay or something?"

Caught me completely by surprise, I'll say that. I said, "No, why?" Then he told me that BUFU was also shorthand slang for . . .

hmmm, how should I put this delicately? *Taking it in the rear*. Get the picture? Not exactly the brand identity we were going for (and, on a personal level, certainly not the image we wanted to put out for ourselves). Of course, we weren't a bunch of *gay haters*, either— after all, we were hoping to make it in the *fashion* industry! But that wasn't what we were about, so we had to look at it again and that's when we changed things up to FUBU: same message, same cool-sounding acronym, even the same letters—only without any confusion over any double-meaning.

From hats, I moved back into t-shirts—this time with two simple designs I'd come up with to support the FUBU name. We used a lot of purple t-shirt blanks, which I thought would really get noticed. Nobody was using purple back then, so even something as simple as a color choice played an important role in building our brand. One design was our name done up in a distinctive script, and the other was a popping FB logo. Back in the early 1990s, you might remember, designers were starting to put their names and logos on their clothes in a big way. It wasn't just a no-frills Lacoste alligator on the chest, or a subtle Polo logo on a cuff, it was a regular billboard, so this was our way to get our name out there and call attention to our line. Here again, we weren't a line in any kind of traditional sense. Nobody knew our name until we put it out there. Our t-shirts were made from seconds that I bought cheap— for about $1 each. They were nice enough, but there was nothing to set them apart, other than their *purple* color or our logo we'd emblazon across the front. That is, until I went to three professional embroiderers and moved our key designs from silk-screening to embroidery. Nobody was doing embroidery back then, so that made us really stand out.

Our whole idea was to offer quality clothes, at a price kids could afford. That was the extent of our marketing strategy. Our target customers were our friends. Their pockets ran about as deep as ours, but so did their desire to wear something stylish. They also wanted to be in on something, to belong to whatever it was we were putting out.

I don't mean to make it sound like FUBU was some overnight sensation. Like I said, we didn't just happen. There was a steady progression, from selling Carhart and Levi's and Super Soakers from the back of my van at concerts and marches and hip-hop shows, to making and slinging those first silk-screened shirts (I had a good run with a batch of Mike Tyson shirts, now that I look back on it), to selling through my first duffel bag of tie-top hats outside the Coliseum Mall, to taking a booth at the Black Expo and trying to kick-start sales to the next level, to the company we are today. But this was the jumpstart. This was us in our *item* stage. This was us on our way to the *label* phase.

We had some help along the way, and we learned a thing or two while we were at it. The biggest thing we learned was that things rarely go according to plan, especially when you're just starting out. Seems obvious, but you'd be surprised how many entrepreneurs are caught short when they're caught by surprise. You can analyze your situation until you're bleary-eyed, but you can't read the market until you're in. You can trust your gut, but your gut can only take you so far. At some point, you've got to respond—and how you respond puts a stamp on everything that happens next.

Hang It Up

One of my priorities at the front end of our FUBU launch was attaching the right label to our product. I spent a lot of time on this, because back then a lot of clothing companies were paying extra attention to their labels. That was the trend, which in some ways led directly to the way designers started billboarding their names in big letters on the clothes themselves. In this way, and in so many others, the fashion industry was moving away from a simple identifying piece of fabric sewn into the back of the collar or inside a pant waist and starting to experiment with big, colorful, attention-grabbing labels, whether they were hung from the garment or sewn directly into them. It was a sign of the times—literally!— and as labels went, they were really, *really* loud. You could see some of these hang tags from clear across the store, before you'd even get a good look at the garment, and I wanted to make sure our labels popped in an ever-crowding field.

I knew the look of our hang tag would say a lot about our line, so I was careful to get it just right. At the time, there was a popular urban clothing designer named Karl Kani, doing some interesting things with his hang tags, so I stole a page from his book. Actually, let's not say I *stole* it. In the fashion industry, we get *inspired* by other designers, so let's go with that. Karl Kani put his picture on his tags, so I figured we'd put our picture on the FUBU tags. (Wasn't exactly the most sophisticated piece of market research, but hey . . . what did I know?) We got this great picture of the four of us—me, Keith, J and Carl—staring straight at the camera and looking like we were posing for a mug shot. Really, we looked pretty menacing, and the image of four black kids, glaring back at you like some thug rappers, was a real contrast to the

vaguely European, vaguely effeminate looks of the other designers on the scene. We'd be the four faces of FUBU, and each of us
would give the brand a different spin. Carl would be the smooth
one. J was slick. Keith had a swagger to him, and I came off as the
mild-mannered guy next door.

It might have been a bit much, to slap our mugs on those tags
and build ourselves into the FUBU brand, but I felt it was important. It fit with our name and our message. We were out there, living on those same streets as our target customers. We were going
to the same clubs, drinking the same champagne, aspiring to the
same things. And so, it made absolute sense that they should see us,
and know us, and get that we cared about what we were selling. We
were walking the walk, same as them.

In the end, those tags made us stars—in a way. People started
to know us— in a way. All of a sudden, we were the FUBU guys. All
of a sudden, we were out in front, representing. Guess you could
say we made ourselves the poster boys for our own movement.
Kids felt like they could talk to us when they saw us in the clubs.
We had a good feel for our market before this, but now we had an
even better feel, because the market reached back out to us and
told us what it was feeling. The carry-over benefit to our business
was that customers felt that by buying our stuff they were helping
us out, and that we in turn understood their needs, their style, their
passion. There was a direct line between us—a lifeline, really, as we
looked to build that all-important brand loyalty we'd need to see
us through the long haul.

Branded!

*"Brands are the express
checkout for people living their
lives at ever increasing speed."*

—Brandweek

JUST ONE IDEA
The Thick 'n Sweet Casebook – Vol. III

Sometimes, things don't go like you planned. Sometimes they go just a little like you planned, but you're far enough from your expectations that you have to rethink the whole deal. And sometimes, you're so far off target you wonder what the hell you were aiming for in the first place.

Point is, the best ideas can have all kinds of holes in them, only you won't know there are holes until you spring a leak. That's why all these big-time companies spend all that big-time money on focus groups and test-marketing strategies, to plug those holes before going forward with a new product launch. But when you're going at it in a mom 'n pop way, you don't have the budget for any of that. It becomes more of a trial-and-error deal. You try it one way and see how it goes—and then, if doesn't go your way, you change it up and take a new approach.

You put it out there, whatever it is you're doing or making or selling, and hope like crazy it floats.

One day, you might look up and realize the viral marketing push you were counting on isn't likely to happen, or, the word of mouth you were anticipating is sickeningly silent, or, the only buzz attached to your business is coming from a lone fluorescent light bulb on the loading dock of the warehouse space you couldn't really afford—and now, apparently, you don't really need.

The scrap heap of failed business plans is piled high with disappointments and miscalculations, so let's not get ahead of ourselves in the maple syrup business and start counting our money before we earn it. Here at our hypothetical Thick 'n Sweet headquarters, we've been mapping out a business on the back of a slightly raunchy but relatively simple idea, hoping to expand the maple syrup market in such a way that we might sell a new syrup line to horny, hungry young adult males. Our success hinges on our ability to turn these horn dogs into customers, to get them ogling our hot, syrupy models in such a way that they can't imagine eating breakfast without our Thick 'n Sweet syrup slathered all over their pancakes and waffles. So far, so good: we've got the recipe cooking. We're ready to rock our poppin' label. Our risqué posters are rolled and ready to hand out all over town, reinforcing our high-concept idea to hire a couple of hot, good-natured models and pour syrup all over their hot, good-natured bodies in such a way that it promotes the syrup. (Doesn't get much simpler than that, does it?)

Our signature is in our name, Thick 'n Sweet, which is meant to suggest the syrup itself, and at the same time remind our target customers of the hot, juicy, sweet images from our marketing campaign, with all those hot, juicy, thick, and sweet ladies. The strategy here is that while most maple syrup purchases are made by women, who tend to do the grocery shopping in most American households, the product itself is most typically consumed by the young, adult males we're hoping to reach. This is the nut of our business plan—to look past the moms and wives who buy this stuff and market a line of syrup directly to the guys who are eating it. It's like an end-around play in football. We run wide of the interference in the middle of the field and hope to catch some daylight on the sidelines, where there's a whole lot less traffic.

Seems like the makings of a sure-fire hit, right? Well, not so fast ... Let's imagine we've hit a bump along the way. Let's consider what our launch might look like when we start to realize some stores won't carry our product. More to the point, let's look at the reasons we might get a less-than-welcome reception with some local establishments. Remember, the distribution end is a little beyond our control, so realistically we can't count on restaurants or bodegas or other outlets to stock our merchandise. That's up to the gods of retail, and they're a hard-to-figure bunch, so it's not unreasonable to expect a little resistance in this area. We might have expected as much, but our head was filled with all that money, and all those images of hot, syrupy girls that maybe we didn't think things all the way through. But at this stage in our product development, we might start hearing that the same down-and-dirty advertising we believed would get our product noticed leaves certain merchants cold, which means we might be cutting off some important avenues of distribution. Something to think about and to weigh against the perceived value of our edgy campaign.

Let's say we've run into a stiff arm from some straight-laced restaurateurs or coffee shop proprietors, who might want to present syrup in a more wholesome way. This is understandable, I guess. After all, it's *their* business, *their* establishment. Doesn't help us all that much, but it's understandable. And it's understandable that we might hit some resistance from church groups and other conservative organizations if we tried to push our product in Bible Belt markets.

In our own backyards, though, it's possible we'll get some push back from reluctant moms, who are doing the buying for their red-blooded, syrup-loving teenage sons, and who think the representation of women in our marketing campaign is derogatory and demeaning. Here again, their objections are understandable. Unfortunate, but understandable. Still, all is not necessarily lost; if we keep at it we're bound to find a bunch of appropriate outlets willing to offer some type of exclusive on an interesting new product that manages to deliver in the quality department—and, we're sure to hit our target market eventually, after these first few misses.

But then again we might not, and here we bump into one of the toughest things you'll ever have to do as an upstart businessperson: shift gears. What seems like a great idea one moment can be a dud the next, even if it was the very idea that got you thinking in this direction in the first place. Sometimes, you have to let one strategy go, and replace it quickly with another. It might occur to us at some midpoint in our new product launch that it could be an effective strategy to contrast our controversial, raunchy approach with a more folksy, traditional campaign to peddle grandmother's maple syrup recipe.

Stay with me on this: let's say your grandmother is active in her church. Let's say that church is located on Farmers Boulevard, back in my old neighborhood. Or maybe that's where she lives. Anyway, you want to call attention to this whole other part of town, where maybe things are more family oriented, more traditional. You can go a whole other way with this product and call it "Grandma's Farmers Boulevard Best," and then you're set up for a much more family-friendly campaign. Yeah, it's a whole different appeal, a whole different approach—and one that looks nothing like your initial hook. With this latest move, you're inching into state fair and family picnic territory; with the first move, you were moving into homeboy fantasy. Can't say for sure which one will work, but they're both worth considering, don't you think? One's a little nasty and out there. One's a little safe and predictable. Same goal, to sell the hell out of this stuff, but you've set out two very different paths to reach that goal, and if you're smart you'll consider what you gain and what you risk by heading down either road.

Are we there yet? Not so fast. I realize I'm mixing my sports metaphors here, and that I'm a little all over the place in my thinking, but that's how it often goes when you're trying to get a new product off the ground. You try everything on and see what fits. You scramble until you hit on the right formula. You set off after one idea to get you going, and you might hit on a completely different idea to see you through.

I'm not suggesting here that we abandon our Thick 'n Sweet concept just yet, only that we might need to retool a bit. After all, it might turn out that our initial, steamy campaign is most appropriate in, say, a college town or, maybe, a fringe neighborhood about to turn to the good, thanks to some redevelopment or gentrification.

Think it through with me: clubs and pubs catering to young adults are more likely to put up your posters of syrupy models than a tavern in a conservative, blue-collar community. Fraternity houses and other school organizations are more likely to host product-launch parties and giveaway events than traditional, Main Street-type establishments. And, young adult males are more likely to display the down 'n dirty posters in their dorm rooms than they are in their bedrooms at home, where a mom and maybe a little sister is looking over their shoulder.

The key to our successful launch, or any subsequent relaunch after an initial push appears to have missed its mark, might just be in recognizing the value of an anything-goes college environment over a more conservative, community. Or, maybe it's the other way around; maybe the conservative approach will turn out to be the best approach, even if it pits us directly against the more established, more traditional syrup brands. Either way, we've got to know our market and tailor our campaign accordingly.

There's no fly in the syrup just yet. The Thick 'n Sweet board is still pumped about its prospects—and there's still every reason for you to be excited as well. But we're at the stage in our development where we need to cover our bets. The strategy going forward, then, is to keep two trains running for as long as possible. We'll continue to test and refine our syrup recipe, to make sure we've got a winning product to take to market. We'll continue to talk to bottlers and packagers, looking for affordable and creative ways to present our product to consumers. And, for the time being at least, we'll hold off on committing to a name and logo until we have a chance to properly test each train as it leaves the station. On one of those tracks, we'll continue with our original concept, perhaps focusing our attention on a college town or a hip, young community. At the same time, we'll continue to look at other, more old-fashioned opportunities, introducing our syrup at church picnics or pancake breakfasts. We'll play both ends for as long as we can, until we either meet in the middle or make the decision to lean one way or another.

Yeah, we might have met a little resistance. Yeah, our sure-fire concept might not be such a sure thing once we're up and running. But we've still got a winning product to take to market—and the truly visionary entrepreneur won't be derailed by a couple of set-backs or slip ups. We'll keep at it until we get it right.

Branded!

*"When you think of the blur of all the brands that are out there,
the ones you believe in and the ones you remember,
like Chanel and Armani, are the ones that stand for something.
Fashion is about establishing an image that consumers can
adapt to their own individuality. And it's an image
that can change, that can evolve.
It doesn't reinvent itself every two years."*

—Ralph Lauren

SIX
Flow

There wasn't much in the way of positive role modeling in my 'hood when I was a kid. It's not like there were too many adults running around in suits with briefcases, chasing serious paper in any kind of serious way. In my case there was my mother, and that was about it.

My father disappeared on us early. He was around for a while, until I was about ten, but he didn't exactly set the best example. He just left. When I was old enough to figure him out, I realized he was all talk. He lied to me. He lied to my mother. He lied left and right and all around. By the time I was twelve, I'd written him off, but I suppose I picked up a trait or two before he was gone. He'd come to this country on his own as a teenager, from Trinidad, and this alone told me he was motivated and adventurous and maybe even hard working. Turns out I'm cut the same way, only I'm determined to keep these good traits working for me—not because I looked up to my father and tried to model my behavior after his, but because it's in my blood. I come by it naturally. My father was motivated in a deceitful, cutting-corners sort of way. I was motivated in a hard-charging, think-for-yourself, do-the-right-thing-and-if-you-don't-make-sure-you-don't-get-caught sort of way.

That part comes from my mother. She was cool. (Still is, by the way.) One of the reasons I made relatively good choices when

I was a kid was because I didn't want to have to look my mother in the face and tell her I'd done something stupid. That look of disappointment? That tilt or shake of her head that told me I'd let her down or embarrassed her in any way? Man, that to me was worse than any punishment I'd get if I ended up in jail.

Find Your Path, Walk Your Path

I didn't always make the *best* choices, of course, but they were pretty good choices, considering my options, and considering what paths some of my friends were choosing. It's not like I could walk around my neighborhood and find too many "young urban professionals," a label marketing types would use soon enough. But the thought of getting the disapproval of this good woman was enough to set any kid straight, so for the most part I stayed out of trouble. It killed me to disappoint her—doesn't mean I didn't disappoint her from time to time, but I hated it.

Hands down, my mother was the most dominant influence of my childhood. She was proud and fiercely determined. Plus, she was a beautiful woman. (Once again, she still is, by the way.) Before I came along, she competed in the Miss Black America contest, so this right here tells you something. She worked at the Playboy Club in New York, as one of the first African-American hostesses. Tells you something, too. She was also a terrific jazz dancer. Mostly, though, she was a hard worker, sometimes running back and forth between two and three jobs, and a super-talented seamstress. This was one of her many sidelines—and she taught me to always have a sideline. "You make a living with your day job," she used to say. "You make money with what you got going on the side."

Another one of her things was to teach me to be leery of whatever people were selling. Companies, politicians, individuals on the street . . . didn't matter. Long as someone or some thing was putting someone or something out there, I needed to understand it for what it was. I needed to look out for the kind of "over-branding" you sometimes see in the marketplace. You know, people who walk around saying, "I own this and I own that." People who call attention to themselves and their accomplishments. It cut the same way for businesses, trying to over-promise a certain result if I used a certain product. That kind of thing just didn't fly with my mother, who was all about letting your actions and talents and service speak for themselves.

Okay, so that was all theoretical. On a more practical level, she also taught me my way around a sewing machine, which didn't strike me as any kind of business opportunity at first— just a way to make something for yourself that you didn't have the money to buy in the store. Wasn't any shame in it either, the way you might think if you were a street kid like me, running with a rough and tumble crowd. It was just a sewing machine, just a way to put two pieces of fabric together and make something out of nothing.

Don't misunderstand, I wasn't some do-good altar boy. I got into my fair share of trouble, but it was rarely the sort of trouble that involved the cops, or guns, or drugs. It was mostly benign, cutting-corners type trouble—and this was bad enough in my mother's eyes. She had a certain way about her, made it so you didn't want her to see you messing up. When it came to her attention that some of my friends were doing drugs and drinking, she put it out there that I was welcome to do the same—but I had to do it with her, in her house. Now, what mother in her right mind tells her teenage son to go out and bring home some powder so they could sniff together? *My* mother. Not because she wanted to get high with me, but because she wanted me to see how foolish and unnecessary it was. She wanted me to feel what it was like to watch someone you love make a big mistake. Mostly, she wanted me to see her doing the same stupid stuff I wanted to do, only on me she knew it wouldn't look so stupid. This doesn't mean I never drank or smoked or did any of that stuff, but I did a whole lot less because my mother spoiled it for me from the jump.

She had a way of getting me to open up to her about whatever was going on in my life at the time. She loved to set up a jigsaw puzzle on our kitchen table. That was how we spent a lot of our time together. If you've ever done jigsaw puzzles, you'll know there can be some pretty long silences as you sit around and try to figure it all out. But in between those long silences there'd also be some good, serious talks. My mother wasn't the type to dig for clues about what was going on with me, but eventually I got to talking. Whatever it was, it would come out over these puzzles, and my mother wouldn't judge or interrupt. She'd just hear me out. Once in a while, she'd set me straight, but mostly she left me to figure things out for myself. In my last book, I said my mother gave me a lot of rope when I was a kid. It's true; she did. That was her great strength. She gave me enough rope that I could either hang myself with it or use it to lift myself up and out; luckily for me, I chose the latter. The rope she gave me was a kind of freedom, a freedom to make my own choices and learn from my mistakes, and it's a blessing that I found a way to use it as leverage instead of constraint.

I set out these examples here to underline one of my main themes, that we're branded at birth. It's a nature *and* nurture thing.

I caught some of my personality traits from my parents, like they were embedded in my DNA, and I caught a whole bunch more by my mother's good and proud example.

Aim High

One of my mother's strategies was to get me to think big. She used to say, "As long as you're thinking, Daymond, you might as well think big." Makes sense, right? Years later, I'd hear the same thing from Donald Trump and think, *Man, my mother was on it long before the Donald.* I read Trump's book, *The Art of the Deal*, and came away wondering when my mother sat him down for a talking-to, because a lot of what he wrote about was the stuff I grew up with. To reinforce her point about thinking big, she used to keep this big old can opener on the wall of our house, with "Think Big" written on it in big, bold letters. It didn't serve any old purpose but to remind me to set the bar of my potential as high as I could imagine and then rise to meet it.

We didn't have a whole lot of money, but we owned our own house. We had a mortgage on it, but it was ours. We worried about our utility bills from month to month, but we did okay. Sometimes we had to wait in line at the local Con Edison office, to pay the minimum balance on our bill at the last possible moment, with whatever cash we could scrape together. Other times, when we were a little short, we had to heat our bathwater on the stove. I can still remember giving myself sponge baths, standing by the kitchen counter. We got by on a whole lot of eggs and free cheese, as I recall. We bought a lot of stuff with food stamps, but there was no shame in that as far as my mother was concerned. Yeah, it was an entitlement program, but she thought we were entitled to the entitlement, so why think about it? It wasn't a hand out. It was a bridge to get us from where we were to where we needed to be. So we held our heads high and put those stamps to good use.

My mother was the first person I knew who bought in bulk to save money. Nowadays everyone buys in bulk, but she was always out looking for the best deals. She even had us driving into the white neighborhoods to do our shopping, because she always said our money went a little further there. She said this without complaint, which I look back on now and admire—because, of course, most other strapped, hard-working African Americans would have taken this as yet another sign that the system was beating them down. But that's the way of it in the 'hood. We're forced to pay more for less, at the same time we're struggling to get by with less, but rather than grumble about the injustice of it all, my mother just pointed our car to the white neighborhood, where we could use our food stamps to buy our eggs and our chopped meat and whatever else we needed at reasonable prices. She learned how to get along, and I learned by watching.

She worked for a while for American Airlines, which offered another great lesson because the job came with free air travel for immediate family. This meant we got to see the world—at least, a little bit. The only drawback to the free travel was we had to fly standby, so a lot of times we'd have to wait around the airport half the day just to get a seat. Still, it's what we could afford.

Together, me and my mother were great students of human nature. Actually, she was like a graduate student, and I was more like a kid in grade school—but we studied together. Most of that studying came during a period when my mother ran a kind of livery service in our neighborhood. It was something to do to fill the gaps our food stamps and her paychecks couldn't quite cover. Most school nights, we were out in our Eldorado, running commuters from the subway station at 179th Street and Hillside Avenue for 50 cents a fare. We'd pile folks in and drop them off all along Hollis Avenue. It was hard, hustling, monotonous work, but we kept plugging away at it. Night after night, we kept at it. We didn't have a taxi license. We didn't have a sign on the side of our car. My mother just hung out on the corner, scraping together these makeshift carpools, asking folks if they needed rides. She had a few regular customers, but since the subway didn't follow any kind of regular schedule she picked up most of her fares on the fly.

I rode in front, and tried to keep my nose in my homework. Wasn't so easy, trying to concentrate with all the noise and commotion coming from the backseat, and all that hustle and bustle back at the subway station as my mother filled the car for the next trip. But the real lesson came when I closed my book and we had the car to ourselves. My mother would talk and talk . . . about people. She'd say, "Daymond, what did you think about that last gentleman we just dropped off?" And I'd tell her what I thought. There was usually some point she was trying to make, to teach me some kind of lesson. About manners. About style. About conversational skills. Whatever. She pointed out the appearance of her customers, their demeanor. She was big into looking people in the eye, and whenever we dropped off a fare who had made a good point of making eye contact, she was sure to point it out to me. She'd say, "Daymond, that gentleman will be successful because he looks you in the eye."

Neither one of us recognized it at the time, but my mother was teaching me about branding even then—about the ways we carry ourselves that reveal our true character. And once she started pointing this out to me, I started thinking about it and coaching myself to mimic the behavior my mother seemed to admire. I started picking people out of the crowd and watching them, wondering if I did the same things I admired, cringing if I sometimes put out the same signs of weakness. I'd ask myself, *Do you make eye contact? Do you make an effort to engage in conversation? Do you speak in full sentences? Are you polite?* Courtesy was a big thing to my mother, and here she got me thinking about first impressions and lasting impressions and everything in between.

"Doesn't cost you anything to be respectful," she used to tell me, and I had no choice but to agree. Underneath these gentle reminders was the foundation for a lifetime. There was the all-important message that we don't skate through this life on our own. People are watching, and considering, and figuring out if they want to help you get a leg up or if they want to go out of their way to keep you down.

Best to do what you can to keep on the world's good side. My mother taught me that.

Finding the Mood

In the clothing business, a lot of designers look to what we call mood boards to help us determine the direction of a new line. A mood board is a collection of cut-outs and clippings, drawings and photos, all bunched together in such a way that designers can get a feeling for the line they're about to develop. It's like a cheat sheet, only there's no cutting corners or ripping off established clothing lines. The idea is to soak in what's out there, to immerse your design team in the sense and feel and imagery you're hoping to invoke, to reach for the right mood and see what happens.

At FUBU, I never really put one of these boards together myself, but once we were up and running we had people collect a bunch of these images, same as every other spot. And now, all these years later, we still go at it the same way. Let's say we're looking at an Excalibur theme for one season, with swords and dragons and suits of armor, or maybe we're thinking of a peacock theme, with bright colors, all spread out like plumage. Whatever motif we're kicking around, we page through a bunch of magazines and grab all these pictures and snatches of fabric, and put them together on this one big board so we can look at them all at once and really develop a feel for it. They do the same type of thing in the music industry, and in advertising. They do it in set design and costume design departments out in Hollywood, and architects reach for their own set of impulses when they're designing a new building.

But in fashion, we've got these mood boards, and I mention them here for the way they reinforce how I tried to present myself as an individual, growing up. It's all about the flow, man. The sense and feel. The theme . . . how it all comes together, all at once. These days, one of our people might come up with an idea for a line of clothing inspired by the 1930s, so we'll do a mood board pulling together different images from the period. Cars, speakeasies, movie stills . . . whatever we can find. Hats, ties and accessories, and one and on. Once the board's complete, it goes up in a prominent way in our studio, so our designers can study it and immerse themselves in it. Doesn't mean they'll be pulling any of their designs directly from these images. Doesn't mean you're out to develop a carbon-copy of the period. What you're looking for, really, is a way to build on the spirit and emotion of those older styles to come up with a fresh new take.

Each season, four times a year, we'll have a new theme. Like I wrote earlier, it turned out that out that our traditional four-season selling cycle didn't always work in our favor, especially once we were up and running. But that was our model, so we kept at it, and during some of those seasons we'd have more than one theme working for us, because you can't put all your eggs in one basket. It's a hit-or-miss business, so you don't want to miss too often—and, when you do, it's nice to have another shot, a backup. Usually, we're selling six months out, which means that in winter we're selling summer, and in summer we're selling winter. That means we have to get these mood boards to our salespeople, too, so they can get inspired by what inspired us in the design, and maybe pass it on to our retailers, and find a way to get past the fact that we're always in the wrong time of year.

In the beginning, I'd just rip out a bunch of pages from a magazine and hand them to one of our designers. I'd say, "Give me something like that." But after a while I figured it out. Somewhere in there it occurred to me that we could do well with a military-inspired line, so I started pulling all these images from the Iraqi war and feeding them to our designers. They looked at me like I was crazy, like I wanted them to come up with a line of fatigues, but after a while they got it and came up with a line that matched what was going on overseas with the street sensibility we wanted to reinforce back home, which translated into a jean jacket with epaulets, for example. It had four pockets, and it looked really interesting. Like nothing else you could find in the stores. Or a hoodie with reinforced pads at the elbows, to suggest a more rugged feel. Also interesting. We even dressed the garment up with a D-ring, so you could hook your keys to it.

The whole process makes me think we should slap some of these mood boards together in our personal lives. You know, just a collage of your life—or maybe the life you imagine. The things you like to do, the places you like to visit, the music you like to listen to. Like all that stuff people put on their Facebook profiles, only here it would be image driven. Aspirational. The stuff we're reaching for instead of just the stuff we already have. There can be a picture of this guy hanging out with his father, maybe fishing or playing checkers. There can be another picture of him working out at the gym, and one of him playing touch football with his boys. Maybe there's a shot of him volunteering at a homeless shelter, or taking care of his mother or grandmother, or hanging at some club surrounded by a bunch of beautiful women. If he's an extreme-adventure type, there'd be shots of him surfing, or hang-gliding, or mountain climbing . . . whatever. And, if he's more of a stay-at-home type but wants people to see him as an outdoorsy, thrill-seeker type, there'd be shots of other people having these extreme adventures.

Think about creating one of these for yourself and it forces you to figure out a few things. Where are you in your life right now? Where do you want to be this time next year? Or, in five years? What kinds of things do you really want out of life? What kinds of people do you want to associate with? It goes back to that "Think Big" can opener from my mother's house. If you do it right you've got something to shoot for—a mix of how you are, how you see yourself, and how you'd like to be seen.

Calling-Card Tricks

Without really realizing it, and without really meaning to, my mother taught me to think creatively in my approach to business—to mix things up in such a way that people couldn't help but notice me. It's an outgrowth of the "think big" message she drummed into me early on, and it's helped me develop my own hit list of branding tricks to help call attention to my efforts.

I'll share some of them here:

- *Use blind embossing on your business cards.* You know, the kind with the raised lettering the color of the card itself. It might not work in every industry, because it's a little out there and funky, but if you're in a creative field, your business card should announce your creativity. The blind-embossing technique can be an effective grabber, because it forces people to pay just a little more attention to who you are and what you're about. You don't see it right away, and then you do—kind of like the way you want to sneak up on people, like a pleasant surprise.

- *Make your business cards a little larger (or, a little smaller) than everyone else's.* Another calling-card tip. Basically, the key point here is that you don't want to be put in the same box with your competitors. Most people reach for the same, cookie-cutter card for themselves, but an oversized card will help you stand out—literally and figuratively. Even if it's just a little larger than the others in the pile, or a little louder, or printed on brighter color stock, or heavier, linen paper, it'll get noticed. The inverse also applies. If your card is slightly smaller than the other cards in someone's collection, yours will invariably wind up on top.

- *Embed your picture in your e-mails.* It might seem cheesy, like those real estate ads you see on the backs of carts at the supermarket, but it's an effective reinforcer. Or, if you don't want to send a photo, use your company logo or some other colorful illustration to help your message "pop" off the screen. Unfortunately, you can't do this on your BlackBerry, and it can be tough to set up one of these personalized e-mails on other handheld devices, but take the time to design a signature look for your standard e-mails, and you'll definitely see the results.

- *Be your own secretary.* This trick has been used so often it's almost a cliché, but it's simple and effective. If it's just you calling on clients or soliciting opportunities, disguise your voice when answering or placing a call. Act the part. Say something like, "Is so-and-so in for Daymond John?"—and then come back on the line as yourself. Answer, "Daymond John's line, how can I help you?"—and then put the call through. It gives the appearance that you're in a position of importance, and it helps you show that you're available, but not *fully* available, all at once.

- *Look the part.* This is a big one on my list. Clean nails, clean shoes, fine clothes . . . it all goes a long way towards a powerful first impression. Even if you don't have a lot of money, find a way to dress for success. (Hey, a pocket square only costs a couple bucks!) Be manicured and crisp. Invest in a decent wardrobe. It doesn't have to break the bank. Two or three pairs of pants, two or three jackets, and a bunch of different shirts and ties are enough to get you by when you're just starting out. But shoes and nails are crucial—they're the first places people tend to look when they're sizing someone up for the first time. Make sure you're up to it.

- *If you're out raising money, don't wear expensive jewelry.* You'd be surprised how many people are turned away by bankers or investors when they come calling behind a flashy new suit or an outrageous piece of bling. Big mistake. Bankers and accountants tend to be extremely conservative, and their style of dress and fashion is a reflection of that. As a general rule, they'll wear tight, conservative suits—and expect you to do the same. You might appear frivolous if you come in wearing a loose-fitting suit, and people of means certainly won't want to loan you money or invest in your business if it appears you squander your money on fancy jewelry. Play it down.

- *Seek a listing-friendly name.* Again, one of the oldest tricks in the phone book, but there's a reason there are so many companies called Acme, or Aardvark Appliances, or AAA this or that—it puts you at the top of the list, alphabetically speaking. When you're starting out, you're looking for every edge, and here you can give yourself a running start on the competition.

- *Dress your packages and mailings for success.* Pay the extra money to send a package by FedEx or UPS—not because it absolutely, positively has to get there overnight, but because your package will arrive with a certain amount of attention and fanfare. The surest way to get past a secretary or assistant is with an important package. Or, if a pricey overnight package seems excessive, place your note or resume in a big, square, fancy envelope—the kind you might use for a wedding invitation. If your handwriting is lousy, ask a friend to address it for you in attractive script.

- *Post-it Up.* I always pay attention when I get a document in the mail that's been dotted by yellow Post-it notes. Even if it just says something throwaway, like "Hey, Daymond, take a look!" It tells me that the sender took the time to think of me—that it's not some mass mailing. It makes it personal and gives the appearance that it came from a friend.

The bottom line is to call attention to yourself in appropriate ways. Think big, like my mother always said, and know that the only way to get your message across is to get your message across—because, hey, if the person you're looking to sell or impress doesn't notice you, you're nowhere.

Branded!

"Customers must recognize that you stand for something."

—Howard Schultz

SEVEN
Making Movies, Building Brands

It took a while to get the FUBU brand the way I wanted it. Actually, it would be more accurate to say it took a while to figure how to build and manage the brand—or to even recognize that's where my focus should have been. I wasn't thinking in terms of *branding* when we got this thing going. I wasn't thinking in any kind of long-term way. My focus was on selling shirts. Lots of them. With any luck, I'd sell through my first line and get started on another. I'd keep rolling this way until I had my million bucks. Then I'd worry about what to do next. That was the extent of my business plan, but then that *item-label-brand-lifestyle* light bulb switched on and I got to thinking there was something bigger going on here. At least, there *could* be something bigger, if I played it right—so I played it, and played it, and played it some more. It wasn't until we hit some growing pains, though, that I even allowed myself to think in any kind of big-picture way.

Here, the big-picture phrase really applies, because over the years I've come to see a lot of similarities between making movies and starting a business. It's all connected. Let me explain: when someone pitches me an idea for a new venture, I'll break it down and say, "Alright, but where's the movie?" That's become a real catchphrase in our office. *Where's the movie?* I put that out there all the time. Same goes for when I'm pitching an idea to someone else. I have to see it, up there on the big screen of my imagination, before I can understand it as any kind of viable business. I'm betting I'm like a lot of people in this way. Hey, I'm a child of the video generation. I have to *see* something in order to get my head around it. I have to connect it to some kind of story, with a beginning, middle and end, and I have to have some idea how things are going go before they get going. I have to have a frame of reference.

Where's the movie? I look for it in every business plan, every new clothing line we consider, every opportunity. Sound crazy? Well, maybe it is, but we live in a visual society. It's all image driven, and story driven. Anyway, that's how it is for me—and for a lot of people, I'm betting. See, young people especially have been raised on music videos, quick-cut, 15-second television spots, and eye-popping billboards and commercial art in such a way that we need to *see* something in order to understand it. We'll see this more and more as the next generation steps up and starts to exert its buying power on our national bottom line. I have a ridiculously short attention span, and if you're out to sell me on an idea or a concept, it had better be a *hot* idea and a *high* concept—because if it's anything less I just won't have the patience for it. I need to *see* it and *get* it right away, otherwise I'm just not interested. I'm on to the next thing—and if *I'm* on to the next thing, you can be sure any potential customer or investor is long gone by the time I figure it out.

That's what I mean by making a movie out of your new business ideas. A movie, I have time for. A movie, I can understand. A movie, I can get behind—straight out of the chute. So tell me the *story* of what you're trying to sell, or build, or whatever. Tell me *your* story and how you came to this venture, this concept, this passion. Tell me where it begins and how it ends. Tell me what things might look like in preproduction, how you'll *cast* your business plan, how you plan to *shoot* it, or execute on your idea, and where you want to be when your movie finally opens. (Hey, if you're really feeling it, you can tell me what the *sequel* might look like.) Play it all out in your head and find a way to download it into mine, and then maybe I'll sign on to it.

Then maybe you'll find your audience.

I didn't think about business in just these terms, back when we were getting FUBU off the ground, but all those movie elements were in place. It just happened that way, I guess. But the FUBU movie was there, all along. We had our high-concept story: a line of clothes for inner city kids and rappers and music industry people, designed by inner city kids who loved the clothes and the lifestyle they represented and who lived and worked and played within the very market they were trying to tap. *For us, by us.* It was right there in our name, for all to see. You didn't have to go looking for it.

Now, after it's all said and done, I think about sitting down and watching the FUBU movie. It's easy to look back and connect all the dots on some of the things we've done, but the real trick is to be a visionary when you're just starting out. Remember, we wrote that movie back in 1992, not 2010.

Back in 1992, we had our set, which for the time being was my mother's house in Queens. Actually, it was my house by this point. She had moved out, and I had been subletting a couple rooms to my boys. very quickly we turned the place into our base of operations. Cleared out all the furniture. Moved our personal stuff into just one or two rooms. Brought in a bunch of sewing machines and cutting tables. It was like our frat house, and factory, and executive office suite—all rolled into one. Definitely, as the principle setting for the movie of our lives, the place was poppin'.

And so we had our basic script, but then we had to go out and *cast* that script and execute on it. We had to scramble to get famous people to wear our clothes—folks whose informal endorsement would lend us some much-needed credibility, star power, and style. And they couldn't just wear it at home, in a casual way; they had to wear it out and about—at openings and premieres, in music videos and concerts, all over the place. Our strategy was to get rappers, athletes and music artists to wear our label whenever and wherever they were out being seen. We used our contacts in the music industry and from the New York club scene to help open some doors for us and make some of these all-important connections. Understand, we didn't have the budget to actually *pay* any of these good people to endorse our product, but we thought we could hustle and finesse them into wearing one of our shirts. We made up a bunch of shirts to hand out just for this purpose. We even had ten high-end shirts in circulation, which we would lend to a star making a special appearance or shooting a video, and which we would then reclaim when the cameras stopped rolling. We had great relationships with hot music video directors, so we were usually able to talk our way onto a set and do our thing. Brand Nubian, Mariah Carey, Old Dirty Bastard, Grand Puba, Busta Rhymes, Miss Jones, Biggie Smalls . . . we managed to get our clothes into videos for all of those artists, and a whole bunch of others, too. Sometimes, we'd pull a shirt from the back of one artist on one set and then race across town to another set and put the same shirt on someone else. We got a lot of use out of those ten shirts. The more success we had in this area, the more we thought to ratchet up the stakes. We kept thinking bigger and bigger, better and better. Mike Tyson—he was someone we thought would represent us well. LL Cool J—another someone we wanted to see in FUBU gear. And on and on. We had this whole wish list of celebrities, ranging from up-and-coming rappers from the neighborhood to A-list movie stars and moguls.

My Rambo *Theory*

A movie phenomenon like Sylvester Stallone's *Rambo* franchise didn't just happen. What we've seen on the screen, from *First Blood*, through all the sequels, are just the finished, fully-realized versions, but they all go back to my *Where's the movie?* approach to any high-concept idea.

Here, around this particular drawing board, a bunch of guys were probably shooting off a bunch of ideas, when somebody said, "Hey, you know what would be great? A movie about some modern day G.I. Joe. Maybe he's a Navy Seal, or a crazy Army ranger. Maybe he's a Vietnam vet, with a couple screws loose. A real wild card. Maybe he doesn't want to be out there, but he's out there."

Very likely, that's all it was at first, before it was fleshed out and story-boarded and whatever other creative turns the producers had to take to move the project along. Like all great ideas, this one had to start somewhere, right? Actually, this one started out as a book, which was also called *First Blood* and published all the way back in 1972, ten years before the movie hit the screens. But it took someone coming across this book and thinking it could be a movie. From here, a bunch of people probably started kicking this one around, and generating some kind of back-story and present-day story arc, and eventually the idea became a script. Probably, there were a couple drafts of that script. Probably, there were a few stops and starts as investors came on board. Somewhere along the way, Stallone became attached, and maybe that required a bunch of rewrites. Maybe there were certain mannerisms or speech patterns of Stallone's that could be written into the story. Maybe Stallone had some ideas of his own that needed to be incorporated. And maybe, once Ted Kotcheff signed on to direct, he had a bunch of ideas of his own.

All kinds of questions must have come up while all these creative types joined forces to create this one movie: where do we shoot this? What's the guy's name? Is he white or black? Does he prevail in the end? Or does he get his head cracked right back? And as those questions got answered, and they started to attach talent to fill all these different roles both in front of the camera and behind the scenes, the thing started to take on a life of its own. It became a *movie*, almost, before it was anywhere close to being an actual movie.

And then, once those cameras started rolling, a whole bunch of other things needed changing. Maybe the weather wasn't cooperating. Maybe one of the lead actors didn't work out. Maybe they shot through their budget after just a few days. Maybe the tension of the story didn't hold together when the director looked at the dailies.

Whatever it is—a movie, a clothing line, a presidential campaign—there are bound to be some unforeseen circumstances, at some point, and the way you grow your movie, your clothing line, your presidential campaign, your relationships with your children, your standing in your community into a successful brand is to navigate those unforeseen circumstances and turn them to some kind of advantage. With any luck, when the Hollywood gods are smiling just right, you wind up making a movie that sticks. That's what happened here, because after *First Blood* came out, kids across the country painted their faces like Stallone and crawl around in the woods, pretending they were in some jungle, clenching a rubber knife between their teeth. The name, Rambo, became synonymous with the kind of tough, loose-cannon, take-no-prisoners persona of John Rambo from the movie, to where some guy, on the dishing-out end of a bar fight, would invariably hear, "Who the hell do you think you are, Rambo?" Or, "I'm gonna go Rambo on 'em"— as a kind of rallying cry to pump yourself up for whatever it was you had to do next. It seeped into the culture, and it didn't go away until the folks behind it made a whole lot of money. Hey, even the knife Rambo carried between his teeth as he made his way through the brush became famous—a must have, for me and my boys.

The lesson: start with the plan, but understand that sometimes that plan is bound to change. All those circumstances beyond your control? You've got to respond to them, and switch things up in a such a way that you move forward, all the while keeping your eyes on the finished product. The movie. The label. The clothes. The campaign. Whatever. It could be your own career, even. You keep that big picture in your head, and the story that goes with it, and sooner or later you'll wrap and send your product out into the marketplace, and people will either line up to see it or they won't. Either it will catch on, or it won't.

Now, here's my Rambo theory. I loved that *First Blood* movie. I loved the first couple sequels. I thought Rambo was one of the coolest cats in the movies. But I'm betting those movies would not have caught on in the same way if Stallone's character had been named, say, John Smith. There's something about the name Rambo that helped the character stand out—like the right product name on the right product. It's the difference between naming your bottled water something innocuous and throwaway, like "Mountain Lake," or something memorable, like "Evian." You can call a bar of soap, "Bar Soap." Or, you can call it "Ivory Snow." One's generic, the other, in your face. One sings; the other doesn't.

Add that memorable name to the great job Sylvester Stallone did with the role, and the great way the story held together, and all that great action, and you have the makings for a blockbuster—and that's the kind of winning combination you need to make noise in almost any field. A whole bunch of things have to fall into place. Some of those things are out of your control, but a great many are directly within your control, and it's up to you to see that they're executed to the fullest, that no opportunity to succeed is left on the table. Then, if the gods don't smile on you, they don't smile on you, but at least you'll know you've put it all out there.

It takes me back to wondering how any manufacturer could ever put a product on the shelves without a carefully considered name. You're making cutting boards? Go out and make the best cutting board you can, at a reasonable price, with the finest materials. But slap a name on the thing. You can't live in that "item" space for too terribly long. In fact, for most products, I can't see living there at all. You'd have to be a moron to put out a product with no identifying marks on it. Even if you're selling fertilizer, you've got to let the world know it's "Joe's Fertilizer," so if your customer is happy with the product and the price and his entire fertilizing experience he'll know where to find you when he's ready for his next sack.

As I look back on our FUBU experience, I have to think our name played a big part in our success. It wasn't just about the clothes. It wasn't just about the lifestyle. It wasn't just about the concept, or the hang tag, or the way me and my partners came across in the clubs and in interviews. It was all of these elements, taken together and mix-mastered in just the right way, and topped off by a memorable, meaningful, *different* name that left no doubt about who we were and what we were about.

Picking and Choosing

The "casting" of the FUBU movie wasn't such a no-brainer for us at the time. In the beginning, we were out there trying to put our clothes on anybody and everybody, but of course it wasn't a completely random deal. Obviously, we couldn't control who wore our stuff, and in the fashion industry you have to take the position that any customer is a good customer. But to be honest, there were certain stars and artists we didn't necessarily want "advertising" our clothes, because the association didn't present our designs in the best possible light. Perfect example: remember that show, *Family Matters*? The one with Jaleel White as this nerdy kid, Steve Urkel? That show was huge, back when FUBU was just coming on the scene, and away from the set I'm sure Jaleel White was a cool, happening young actor who had it going on. No doubt, he was talented. No doubt, folks across the country were looking up to him in an admiring way—young people in particular. But Jaleel White was so closely associated with that nerdy Urkel character that it wouldn't have been in FUBU's best interest for him to parade around in our clothes. No disrespect to Jaleel, but it would have stamped us a certain way, and we trying to stamp ourselves a whole other way.

Now, it never came up. This is just a hypothetical situation to help me make my point. Jaleel White never reached out to us or asked us to comp him some FUBU clothes, but if he had, we would have thought long and hard about it before accepting his "endorsement," even in an informal way. We would have weighed the positive attention we might have received just from getting our clothes noticed and talked about, against any negative associations that might have come up because people might think our stuff was something the Urkel character might wear.

Generally speaking, we were in a good position, in terms of reaching out to the right artist, to give us the right push. Where we grew up, in Hollis, Queens, there were a whole bunch of rappers and hip-hop artists. There was LL Cool J. There was Hype Williams, the top music video director of the day. We could have gone any number of ways, reaching out to any number of contacts. Our strategy was to steer clear of the so-called "backpack" rappers, artists like A Tribe Called Quest, Jungle Brothers, and De La Soul. It wasn't our first choice to throw in with this bunch, because that wasn't the image we wanted to present. I liked these artists well enough, but they weren't about the clothes, the image, the bling. Instead, we were looking for artists with a little more edge to them—a little more juice and style—so we only went after the high-gloss rappers who talked about opulence and excess and decadence in their rhymes. The hardcore rappers, they were more our style. They were where we wanted to be, on the high end—and at the time, LL was the high end of the high end.

The trouble with LL, early on, was he didn't like some of our

clothes. He was up front about it. Specifically, he didn't like how
we were using purple as our primary accent color in our first line of
shirts. This was the time I hinted at earlier on in these pages, when
our distinctive color almost came back to bite us. The designs he
liked just fine; the purple just didn't do it for him. He said it didn't
match his sneakers, and this created a bit of a problem. I got where
he was coming from on this, because I was the same way, so I knew
we couldn't move him off that view just by pushing. We had to take
another approach. In every other respect LL was perfect for us,
and he was willing to get behind us and go hard. The purple accent
was also important for us, because no one else was using that color
in such a prominent way. Very quickly, it had become our signature color. We even had a couple shirts that were full-on purple. It
wasn't just an accent color, it was the whole shirt. So the dilemma
was, how do you attach a star like LL Cool J to an upstart clothing
line that was using a color he didn't like?

My first thought was to go out and buy LL a bunch of purple
sneakers. I'd custom design them if I had to. But he was like me
about his kicks, and I knew that wasn't going to work, so going back
to my movie analogy I guess you can say we hit the editing room.
Just like happens with movies, we had to rewrite the script a little
bit, and reshoot a couple scenes, because things weren't turning
out the way we planned. We had LL all lined up, but then we had
to design another couple shirts he'd be comfortable wearing—and
all of a sudden our movie had a different look to it. We filed this
in the "Oh-well-what-are-you-gonna-do?" category and found a
way to make it work. Hey, I'm sure *Jaws* didn't exactly unfold the
way Steven Spielberg had it pictured in his head. You know, maybe
the mechanical shark didn't work the way he wanted it to work,

or maybe the weather didn't cooperate when he was shooting his exteriors. Sometimes, you just have to wing it, and here we were, winging it, hoping for the best.

Meanwhile, nobody's really aware of the production of the "movie," as it gets underway. These days, it's not even a full-blown movie anymore. It's more like a video—three and a half minutes to sell your story, your vision, your brand. In some circles, it's an even quicker hit—a "tweet," the essence of who you are and what you're about reduced to 140 characters or less. It's all telegraphed and telescoped and distilled into a tiny, digestible piece. But whatever form it takes, however long or short, the folks on the receiving end of your movie or video or tweet, the consumer or the investor or the audience . . . they don't see all this behind-the-scenes stuff. The product just arrives on the shelves or in their face, fully realized. They don't know what's behind it. They just know what they see, what you present. In our case, they didn't know how I turned my house upside down, and filled it with sewing machines, and piece workers. They don't know how I used the equity in my house to ramp up production, how I had everything I owned tied up in the success of this company. All they saw were four kids from Queens, getting going on this new enterprise. On the front end, we were poor and hustling. On the back end, we're driving off in our Mercedes with the girls and the champagne. And the stuff in the middle is all left to the imagination.

I'll tell you, that wasn't how our story was supposed to end. All I wanted, going in to this FUBU deal, was to find a way for me and my boys to make a decent living. The girls and the champagne and the fancy cars? That stuff was an added bonus. I didn't mind it too much when that was how it turned out, but that wasn't our goal.

The way my FUBU movie was supposed to end was people excited about our line, and buying up our clothes, so we could justify making and peddling a second batch. And then a third. And on and on. Eventually, the idea was to move the operation out of my house and into a boutique somewhere in Manhattan. That's all any of us really wanted out of the deal.

And then we went out and changed the stakes.

Making Magic

With FUBU, we are all about the first impression—and we were forced to make a bunch of them. That's how it goes when you're launching a new business, a new product, a new line. You introduce yourself in one way to one group of potential customers or supporters or investors, and then you go out and introduce yourself a whole other way to some other group. You're always making introductions, which means you're always getting a fresh crack to put yourself across. Our thing was to get our name out there, hard, along with our back story and our clothes and anything else that might drive people to buy one of our garments for themselves, or order a whole batch for their stores. We'd hit it as hard as we could, and after that, if we hadn't hit our mark, we'd just hit it again. It started in our own neighborhood, and eventually itgrew to the rest of the city, and then to the region. At some point, we looked up and thought, *Man, this thing could go national if we gave it the right push.*

And so, on our tight budget, we looked to give it the right push. Over and over again, until something pushed back. Or, until we ran out of introductions and first impressions and had to rely on whatever image of our company and our clothes had somehow taken hold.

One of our first big pushes came on the back of a photo shoot we'd done with LL wearing one of our (not purple!) shirts. We ended up placing the ad in a national magazine called *Right On!*, which was what we could afford. Not the biggest national magazine, but a national magazine. We'd already gotten LL to wear our stuff in a couple of his videos, and after that he wore one of our hats in a GAP ad and snuck in a FUBU line in one of his raps: "For us, by us, on the low." That was enough to get us rolling on the cheap.

Next, we made a stack of copies of the ad and took them with us to Vegas, where we thought we'd use them as calling cards. There was a big clothing convention we'd decided to attend, only we didn't have enough money to purchase a booth or prepare any proper promotional materials. So me and my boys spread out on the convention floor and hustled up business on the back of this ad. We'd show buyers this great shot of LL, wearing our clothes, and then we'd invite them back to our room at the Mirage, where we'd set up some clothing racks and displays. We didn't have a suite or anything, just a standard hotel room, and there were five of us crowded into that one room, but during the day we threw our personal stuff in the closet and made the place look presentable.

The convention was known as the MAGIC show, a twice-yearly event that has lately become a must-attend event for any company looking to launch or highlight a new line of street wear or urban fashion or, really, any forward-looking fashion design. Back then it was more of a traditional show, featuring mainstream designers and manufacturers catering to middle-of-the-road tastes, but we helped change all of that. Over the years, once we started making some money, we had a bigger and bigger presence at these shows. Eventually, we started throwing parties, and these too got bigger

and bigger each year, to where our FUBU events became a highlight of the convention—so much so that now pretty much every
designer and manufacturer looks to host some type of lavish party.
But I don't want to get ahead of myself hear, because our very first
MAGIC experience wasn't like that at all. We basically just snuck
around the place, like "convention crashers."

(Hey, *that's* a movie!)

MAGIC once stood for Men's Apparel Guild in California, but
now it's just MAGIC. That's all. And it's become the leading trade
show for the entry-point fashion industry in the United States.
In a lot of ways, it's come to represent the same opportunity for
manufacturers and designers of street wear and everyday fashions
as New York Fashion Week now represents for couture; it shouts
to the industry what kids and young adults will be wearing for the
next year or so.

I can't say for sure how we got it in our heads that we should be
at that show, or what we were thinking heading out there, but once
the idea hit we were all over it. I still had my mother's stand-by
privileges at American Airlines, so I was able to catch a free flight
out to Los Angeles. The rest of my boys all managed to get out to
L.A. on the cheap, and from there we rented a van and drove back
to Vegas. We didn't take the town by storm, but we lit it up best we
could on our tight budget.

Like I said, we couldn't afford a booth on the convention floor,
but we got our hands on a couple of passes and started freelanc-
ing. We worked that floor like it had our name on it. All around
at the MAGIC trade show, designers were displaying their clothes
in their fancy booths, circulating their fancy business cards and
promotional materials, while we were handing out tear sheets from

Right On! and hoping to lure buyers a couple of miles from the convention hall to our crappy little room at the Mirage. Straight off, people knew us as these fish-out-of-water, street-talking kids from Queens, trying to do business with all these traditional retail clothing and designer types. We stood out, I'll say that.

The first piece of magic at that MAGIC show was that we got anybody at all to follow us back to our room. I'm surprised these cats didn't think we'd jump them as soon as we got them away from the convention crowds. The second and sustaining piece was that we wrote about $300,000 worth of orders, and that was enough to get us started. A little bit more than enough, to tell the truth, because it left us with the daunting task of actually filling those orders, arranging financing, and ordering enough material to fill a small warehouse. In all, we contracted to make about 15,000 garments, which meant we needed to have giant rolls of fabric shipped to the house on Farmers Boulevard and that we'd be working pretty much around the clock. The garments were to be spread fairly evenly over four different items: an embroidered scuba-type jacket, cut from a neoprene material; a sweatshirt; and a polar fleece sweat suit, pants and top. We even caught a break on those scuba jackets, while we were deep into production, when Busta Rhymes put one on in one of his breakthrough videos, and people started asking for it.

In addition, we maxed out our credit cards to buy up as many blanks as we could find, at reasonable prices, and we started to stockpile a bunch of t-shirts and hats tricked out with our logo—to supplement our initial orders.

If you didn't know any better, you could have walked by my house in Hollis at the time and mistaken us for a real business.

We were and we weren't. We had six or seven full-time Latino seamstresses, coming in to work every morning. We had delivery men coming and going all day long. There was heat and haste and hustle all around. It was a residential neighborhood, but we just went about our business. We even had the fire department coming by every couple days, investigating an ongoing complaint from our neighbors about the toxic plume of purple smoke that seemed to hover over my house like a sick *Bat signal*. The smoke was from the way we used to burn our excess materials at the end of each day, because we couldn't afford a dumpster or set it up so the stuff could be removed properly. We set out this big empty oil drum in our backyard, and piled in all these polar fleece remnants, and a whole bunch of other synthetic materials, never thinking we were in violation of any kind of code. After all, this was Queens, and guys used to hang out by these oil drums in junkyards all winter long, burning old tires to keep warm, so I just thought, *Hey, why can't I do the same in my own backyard?*

We weren't exactly poster kids for the Better Business Bureau in our area, the way we ran out of the house every time the fire department banged on our door, but what the hell did we know?

Working the Numbers

I'm not out to tell the entire FUBU story all over again in these pages, but there are a couple relevant highlights that speak to our branding theme. In one, early on, we had to respond to a shift over at MTV, where they started blurring labels and brand names whenever they appeared in music videos, which started happening more and more in the early 1990s. This could have been a devastating move for us, because we were relying on these product-placement videos to keep our name and our clothes out in front of our targeted customers. In fact, it *was* pretty devastating, until we found a way to regroup. Under this new policy, artists could still wear our clothes in their videos, but the FUBU name would be blurred by the network—kind of like how news stations scramble the faces of people they don't want you to recognize. If that happened, we'd still get play on BET and in the clubs, but we'd lose out on all those MTV viewers.

Potentially, this was a serious issue for us, because we'd built all that initial momentum in music videos. And we'd had great success with it too, judging from the way other companies kept hopping aboard the same strategy. It got to where you couldn't flip on MTV without seeing some identifiable clothing item, or car, or champagne, or some other product on prominent display in a music video, so I could see why the execs felt they had to do something. After all, how could they keep asking Coca-Cola and Sony to keep handing over their ad dollars when companies like FUBU and Daimler-Chrysler and Tiffany were getting all that air time for free? But even though I understood the move, I still looked to dance around it because I wasn't about to give up a good thing without a fight. We didn't have any kind of serious advertising budget because we were counting on these videos to get and keep our name out in front, and now these MTV executives pulled the plug on us. Here we'd hustled and developed this great loophole strategy and jumped inside in a big-time way, and now that loophole was threatening to close around us like a noose.

So what did we do? I hit on another end-around strategy, stealing an idea from some other designers that I thought I could bend to our situation in such a way that I'd get a brand-new, scramble-proof logo out of the deal. Here again, *stealing* is probably too harsh a word to describe what I was doing. Better to say I was *inspired* by some of the other trends going on in the fashion industry at the time—specifically, the move by clothing companies like Polo to use the year of their establishment in their designs. Nike did a whole line of Michael Jordan gear just using his uniform number, 23, to signal the Jordan brand, so numbers were very much a part of the design landscape at the time. I started to think there had to be some way to identify our brand with a number, in such a way that the number alone might signal the FUBU line—and, if it was just a number, MTV would have a hard time justifying a move to black it out.

As it turned out, we were selling a lot of hockey jerseys back then, and we were using the number 05 as a default uniform number on those jerseys. After that, we put it on all our shirts. There was no real reason we hit on the number, except I liked the way it looked. I liked that you wouldn't see a professional athlete wearing the same number in quite the same way. Most of all, I liked what the number represented: all of us, in this thing together, creating our own look, our own mystique . . . even our own numbers. I started telling people the number stood for an unnamed fifth FUBU partner. There were the four of us—me, J, Carl and Keith—but there was room at the table for one more, for the FUBU customer, who in some unspoken way was in on every decision we made as a company. You see, For Us, By Us wasn't just some tag line. We took it seriously. We took it to mean we were all in on the same ground floor, with our customer, and that was reinforced by our new 05 logo—a logo MTV couldn't touch, by the way.

Over time, we started using that number on everything we put out. It was a big design element for us, and folks couldn't help but connect that number back to FUBU. (We still reach back for it from time to time.) We didn't have to spell it out for our customers; they just knew, the same way they knew what the letters in our name represented, long after we'd sold through our first line of shirts. It took on a life of its own, and MTV kept airing all these videos with artists wearing our clothes, only now it looked like they were wearing a uniform number so nobody bothered to blur the identifying marks. Now we were back in the game.

That 05 did a whole lot of business for us, and I set it out here as a reminder that you *can* reinvent the wheel, once you get your company rolling. Yeah, you can invest all that time and effort and money into promoting a certain logo, a certain image, but if circumstances pile up in such a way that you need to think about re-investing in a whole new approach, then that's what you need to do. You can't be married to one approach. You've got to mix it up, adapt, and move on.

Get Me Security

Another highlight—and, still, one of my all-time favorite examples of the *guerilla branding* strategies we put in place on our nothing budget—was an ad hoc, street-level campaign we put together on the fly. Let me pull back and explain. There's enormous power and reach in an urban billboard campaign, if you can afford one. Trouble was, back when we were just starting out, we couldn't afford one—although even if we could there might have been an even stronger opportunity laying in wait.

In any case, the idea of making the FUBU name a part of the

landscape was appealing to me, so I scratched my head to come up with ways to "billboard" our name without spending a whole lot of money. What I came up with was simple: security gates. Specifically, those gun-metal pull-down gates New York City merchants use to secure their storefronts when they close up shop for the night. We've all seen these gates. Most of the time, we don't even notice them. More often than not, these gates are public eyesores, so I thought we could solve two problems with one toss by cleaning them up and spray painting the FUBU name across them in a colorful, attention-getting tag. Done right, it could be a win-win strategy —FUBU would benefit, because we'd get to display our name in a prominent, poppin', unexpected way, on the very streets where we were hoping to make our biggest impact; the mom 'n pop storefront owners would benefit as well, because we would power-wash their gates, decorate them, and clean up their neighborhoods.

I hired a couple graffiti artists and priced it out, calculating it would cost about $200 to clean and paint each storefront. Not a whole lot of money, when you think about what you're getting in return. Those gates tended to be down from six or seven o'clock at night until seven or eight o'clock the next morning, which meant we were catching a good chunk of rush hour traffic at each end. Compare that to a couple thousand dollars for a single billboard for just one month, where you might get just as many views, and you can see why I was drawn to this approach.

Of course, the barriers to entry to our barrier-to-entry graffiti campaign was gaining the permission of the individual merchants —but I'm happy to report that our targeted stores almost always signed on, and once they did they stayed with the program. Yeah, they could have painted over our designs and slapped on a design of their own, but each week we'd add another few storefronts to our urban makeover campaign. And for the most part, the store owners kept our design on their gates long after our handshake agreement expired, to where you'd eventually see all kinds of other graffiti markings spray-painted alongside our FUBU name. (Even today, nearly 15 years later, you can still see our faded FUBU markings on dozens of gates all around the city.)

In the end, we painted over 60–70 security gates. You couldn't drive through any New York City neighborhood after seven or eight o'clock at night without seeing the FUBU name, and it was in every respect a successful marketing push. I mention it here because whenever I talk to young entrepreneurs looking to get a jump start on a business opportunity, I point to this security-gate story as an example of how you have to think outside the box if you want to get and keep ahead. Yeah, that line has been beaten into the ground in so many business books it's almost a cliché. *Think outside the box*. Okay, tell me something I *don't* know, right? What does that really mean? To zig when the other guy zags? That's another tired business line. The idea, really, is to go against the grain, to analyze how your competitors are going about *their* business and then see if you can go another way with yours.

Here it's not just that we managed to carve out a street-level campaign without a whole lot of money, because even if we had unlimited funds I can't imagine a more effective, more appropriate strategy. No, the real lesson of our security gate billboards was that you can't *just* throw money at a business plan and expect to see results. In this case all the money in the world wouldn't have bought us the same urban exposure. As it turned out, our makeshift, penny-pinching strategy fit perfectly with our image, our clothes, our name. *For us, by us*. Reinforced in our toughest neighborhoods, our richest neighborhoods, our poorest neighborhoods . . . night after night. You could drive by in a bus or a cab on the way home from work and be reminded of the FUBU brand, in an unlikely, memorable way. We were in the air, and all around.

Can't put a price on that.

The Beauty of Being Black Owned

A central element of our FUBU story was right there in our name: *for us, by us*. You could draw a straight line from that sense of belonging to our first rush of success, and our customers seemed to take these little points of pride in helping a bunch of kids from the neighborhood make good. We hadn't really counted on that, but there's no denying that a big part of our appeal was that we were keeping folks' hard-earned money circulating in our own community. It made sense, I guess. All over New York, you'd see other minority groups rallying round and supporting their own businesses. You'd see it in Chinatown, in Little Italy, in the Hispanic bodegas that dot the streets in almost every neighborhood. There's a great sense of shared purpose that comes with spending money in such a way that you take care of your own. Also, there's a rooting interest you take, when you know your support helps to keep a company going.

It wasn't always that way, at least not in our household. We shopped all over the place when I was a kid. Macy's, D'Agostino's, Radio Shack . . . wherever my mother felt she could get what we need at a price we could afford. The only color my mother saw when she was shopping was green, and the more green she kept in her pocketbook the happier she was with the transaction, but a lot of folks see things through a black-and-white lens. We started to notice that right away. Our customers seemed to respond to the fact that they were giving something back, and we were giving something back, and we were all in this thing together. Yeah, they liked our clothes. But they also liked that they weren't giving money to the white man. They liked that whatever windfall came our way we'd probably pour right back into our own community.

We got some flak about this when we got together with the good people at Samsung—specifically, with our new friends and partners Norman and Bruce Weisfeld. Out of nowhere, we started hearing these negative comments, about how we'd sold out, how FUBU was no longer in our control. But that's not how it was. What happened, plain and simple, was we got to where we needed some distribution to jump-start our growing business. And some capital: we couldn't even buy the materials to fill those first MAGIC orders without someone else's paper. The banks weren't too keen on giving black kids a bunch of money, even with our sound business plan and all those orders. So I started reaching out to other fashion industry investors who were looking to sink some money into a viable start-up operation like FUBU, and that's how I came across the Weisfelds, from Samsung's textile division. They were good guys. Their main business was bubble coats, which meant that for half the year things were kind of slow. They were looking to expand.

I brought my mother along to discuss our deal. I know it probably looked lame, but she was smart. She knew her stuff. She had my back. And at the other end we came away with a deal that was far better than any I could have negotiated for myself—one that anticipated the importance of perception in the marketplace before I recognized it myself. We continued to call our own shots (*we*, meaning me, J, Keith, and Carl), while Samsung became our financial partners. I've got to credit Norman and Bruce for that, because they recognized that being black-owned and black-operated could really distinguish our brand. To their thinking, it was like a seal of approval. It meant we could be trusted. It meant we were out in front, working it—for our own benefit, to be sure, but also for our customers.

Can't put a price on that, either.

Branded!

*"I know some people say, 'Keep your eyes on the prize,'
but I disagree. When your eyes are stuck on the prize,
you're going to keep stumbling and crashing into things.
If you really want to get ahead, you've got to
keep your eyes focused on the path."*

—Russell Simmons

JUST ONE IDEA
The Thick 'n Sweet Casebook – Vol. IV

Okay, so what do you do when you reach the place where a hot idea turns out to be more trouble than its worth? Or when there's just not enough *heat* to get you past the trouble spots in your path?

Well, that depends. For one thing, it depends on the product you've been able to develop on the back of your initial business model. We touched on this earlier, in our imagined case study, but let's revisit it here, now that we've *imagined* we're running into some speed bumps in our development and launch phases. Early on, it didn't matter that the titillating, high-concept marketing campaign came first, and that you developed your product to suit. It didn't matter that your business model was never about bringing a new or innovative recipe to market. Hey, it didn't even matter that you never gave the end-game product a serious thought, because you were in quick-hit, take-the-money-and-run territory. At least, it didn't matter just yet ... but at some point, soon, it will matter most of all. Maybe you're already there in your thinking. Maybe the not-so-warm reception you've received in your initial push has caused you to realize that, in the end, the make or break aspect of your new business launch will be whatever it is you're hoping to sell. How you go about your selling might have been the primary focus, but in our hypothetical "Thick 'n Sweet" launch it's become secondary soon enough.

And so, consider the syrup. Sooner, rather than later. Sooner, as in *now*. It's the only move left to you at this point, if you hope to set things right and pull some kind of business from these stops and starts. You can still rescue this puppy from the scrap heap of new business ideas that never quite got off the ground, but in order to do that you'll need to put some time into an innovative, tastebud-grabbing recipe and see where it takes you.

Yeah, I know, you should have covered some of this ground already. Yeah, I know, this was nowhere near your focus going in, when it was really just about capitalizing on a clever gimmick and having some fun on your way to the bank, but it needs to be your emphasis now. It's the only move left to you at this point, so you'll need to get on it. You see, nothing's ever easy when you're launching a new product or business. If something seems too good to be true, that's because it is. It's a pipedream to think you can map out some fantasy start-up plan and expect the whole deal to go down like it does in your wildest dreams. Doesn't happen that way . . . except, of course, when it does. But when it doesn't, you need to regroup. Refocus. Reimagine.

Chances are, you've spent most of your time on your marketing and packaging, which made sense when you were looking ahead to one kind of launch. You've been too busy trying to convince pretty girls to let you pour syrup all over them to worry about anything else, and I can't really blame you. (Hey, that's where my focus would have been—better believe it!) But now you need to broaden your concept and cast a wider net, since it appears your initial approach might have some holes in it. I mean, if all you've got at this late stage of your product launch is an attention-getting labeland some eye-popping posters and other promotional materials to dress up your winning concept, you might want to fold your tent and move on to the next big idea. However, if you've somehow managed to grow your initial impulse into a product that's got some real and sustainable value to it, you might be inclined to press on. So this is where you'll want to take a step back and pay good and serious attention to the merchandise.

What, exactly, are you selling? Who, exactly, is your competition? What, exactly, is your profit margin on each bottle? And what, exactly, is your break-even point on your initial production run? Up until this point, there was no reason to spend a whole lot of time assessing the maple syrup business in general, in learning and analyzing the field, or making any kind of careful study of successful syrup marketing or pricing strategies. You were out for that quick hit, so you didn't give this kind of groundwork too much thought. You didn't think about patenting your product, or trademarking your name, or finding a way to make sure the proprietary elements of your business plan couldn't be bent or borrowed by anyone else looking to cash in on the same idea.

But that's about to change—because, let's face it, without a slam-dunk, can't-miss promotional campaign *and* a slam-dunk, can't-miss product, you're headed into pet rock territory. By this I mean you'll reach the point where your launch is mostly about the marketing and packaging and hardly at all about what it is you're actually *selling*. Therefore, the syrup: is it generic, forgettable, nothing special? Or, is it distinctive, award winning, mouth-watering? Figure it out, and adjust your next move to match. Are you at the *item* stage of your product development? Is your stuff good enough to justify its own *label*? Do you have the legs and the reach to grow your syrup into a *brand*? And, just how far out is it to think you might someday land at the *lifestyle* level, with a whole line of "Thick 'n Sweet" t-shirts and beach blankets and spatulas to flip the pancakes you'll want to make in order to enjoy your syrup?

I'm reminded here of some of the unremarkable, marketing-driven products from my childhood—one-off items like "Billy Beer," endorsed by President Carter's beer-drinking brother Billy, or "Reggie Bars," a chocolate nut candy endorsed by Yankee great Reggie Jackson. Obviously, nobody cared about the beer or the candy. It was all about the packaging the tie-in campaign, and the celebrity endorsement, but here it looks like we'll have to start thinking about the product. Our "Thick 'n Sweet" syrup will actually have to have some merit to it if we hope to make any kind of dent in the marketplace.

As long as I'm on it, let's recognize that there's a long history of tie-in candy deals, looking to cash in on some fad or phenomenon. There have been *Stars Wars*-themed M&Ms and *Indiana Jones*-themed Snickers bars, and on and on, but in those examples it was never about the candy. It was always about the wrapper, the brand, the tie in. Even a high-end chocolate outfit like Godiva looks to get in on this game, from time to time, as it did recently with a series of *Twilight*-inspired candy bars, only here at least there was a presumed takeaway to the transaction—meaning that the chocolate was actually worth the calories.

Anyway, if you haven't done so already, this is where you'll want to put some money into your recipe. This is where you'll roll up your sleeves, hit the kitchen, and hope inspiration finds you on its own. This is where you'll have to start seeking out local bake-off contests, to hopefully win you and your syrup some followers. Or, arrange for some giveaway, and promotional breakfasts at a prominent diner in town.

There will be a number of next moves available to you at this point, but none of them will be obvious or transparent. Spend some time on this, and think things through. Your initial impulse was just that—an impulse. Now you've got to play things out and see where they take you. One thing seems certain, though: it will no longer do to reposition or rebottle some garden-variety syrup and pass it off as the next big thing. From here on in, you'll have to layer in some distinctive new flavoring, or deploy only healthy ingredients, or find some way to give your item the edge in the marketplace you'd hoped to gain with your raunchy ad campaign. Keep in mind, you can still pursue the raunchy ad campaign if it continues to make sense in certain markets, and it still might make all the difference in your ultimate success, especially if no one else in the syrup game is taking the same approach, but there's got to be some underlying value to what you're doing. There's got to be that Godiva takeaway. Or, it might turn out that your fallback, Farmers Boulevard approach, trying to tap into an older, more traditional market, is really the best way for you to go.

And another thing: if your first attempts at marketing your syrup tell you that it's not post-adolescent frat boy or homeboy-types who tend to do most of the syrup buying in your neighborhood, you've got to find a way to get your product into their hands anyway. After all, they *eat* the stuff, they just don't *buy* it, so you've got to scratch your head on this and figure a way to complete the transaction for them.

Figure it out. And, if nothing seems to work, don't be afraid to put a pin in your efforts and set the whole project aside for a while. Give yourself some distance. Best advice I ever heard (or gave!) was to step back from a series of unexpected roadblocks.

Chill. Re-evaluate. Brush your shoulders off and come back to it in an entirely new way. It just might be that the barriers to entry in the syrup game are too great to support a scattershot, ground-up launch of an untested, undeveloped new item. Maybe there's a better way to capitalize on your initial idea of pouring hot maple syrup on a bunch of hot young models. Let's not give up on your vision just yet. (Because, hey, it's really quite a vision!)

Here's an idea that just might work: instead of looking at it from a manufacturing perspective, why not pursue it as a pure marketing play? Why not reach out to an existing regional brand and see if you might interest them in your campaign? Think about it. Maybe there's a strong line of syrup products out there that just can't seem to catch a break or stand out in a crowded field. Maybe they've got all the elements in place that you were seeking, but they can't get hot. Maybe your idea is just what they're seeking—a fresh, bold way to distinguish their syrup and help tap an untapped market. They've already got a handle on the recipe and the bottling and the distribution. They're just missing the hook—a reason for someone to pick up one of their bottles instead of one of their competitors'.

Do your homework, and you might find just such a company, facing just such a dilemma, and here you'll find your back at the cross-hairs of our professional pursuits and our personal brand. It goes back to what we were talking about earlier on in these pages, about how the way we carry ourselves announces our goals, our dreams, our intentions. If you're setting out to be the guy who calls on some low-level food distributor, hoping to interest him or her in a racy campaign to help promote a slow-selling syrup line, you had better dress the part. If you go in looking like some fleabag promoter, looking to find an outlet for a bunch of swimsuitmodels, chances are you won't really get anywhere. But if you go in dressed like a professional, with a detailed marketing campaign and a practiced pitch outlining your bold, outrageous approach, you just might get a hearing.

If you do, be sure to make a strong presentation, because you'll only get one second-shot here. You've already misfired on the first one, but you can learn from those mistakes as you repitch and reposition your idea.

It might not be the pot of gold at the end of the rainbow you'd imagined going into this enterprise, and it might not present a buildable, sustainable business at the other end of your launch, but it'll be something. Or, not . . . but that won't be the point. The point, after all, is that things don't always play out the way we imagine, at least not on the first pass. You've got to catch a couple breaks along the way—and if you don't, you've got to find a way to make your own breaks. That's pretty much how things went down when we were getting FUBU off the ground. We had a strong idea for a line of clothes. We sold through our first couple runs like nothing at all, but we weren't really getting anywhere. I had some money in my pocket, but that was about it. What I really wanted was a business—but in order to do that I had to try a whole bunch of different approaches. I had to take my initial concept and find a way to fit it into the marketplace.

Ultimately, that's where you'll land on this "Thick 'n Sweet" model. Somewhere between your pie-in-the-sky fantasies and the feet-on-the-ground realities of doing business in the real world.

Just do me one favor: let me know how it goes.

(Oh, and one more: invite me to the photo shoot!)

Branded!

"When the idea came up, I said, 'Are you crazy?
Stick my face on the label of
salad dressing?' And then, of course,
we got the whole idea of exploitation
and how circular it is. Why not, really,
go to the fullest length, and the silliest length,
in exploiting yourself and turn
the proceeds back to the community?"

—Paul Newman

EIGHT
You

Step back from what you do for a living and consider how you come across when you interact with other people. In your professional life, in your personal life, across the board. What a lot of people don't realize is that all these principles of branding and positioning we've been kicking around, of building a name and a reputation in business, of "making movies" to sell your product or vision . . . they apply to character as well. They apply to our *relationships* as well.

They apply to *you*—in every way.

Item-label-brand-lifestyle . . . you can retro-fit most of our relationships into each one of these stages. Personal, professional, and across the board, but we see the connection most clearly with our romantic relationships. You get together, you check each other out and go out on some dates, and all of a sudden you're an item. You hear that phrase all the time, attached to some couple just starting out: "Oh, those two, they're an *item*."

Next, you're going together a while, you become a kind of label. In fact, your friends and family will start to blend your names together, like they do in the gossip section with all these celebrity couples. *Bennifer, Bradjelina, TomKat* . . . whatever. It's almost like the people around you have to come up with a new way of thinking about you, like they've got to slap an actual label on you, now that you're in a relationship. It's no longer just you, it's the two of you, and we've got all these subtle and not-so-subtle shifts in the language to reflect that. It's the short-hand, informal version of putting your initials on a set of hand towels, and it springs up pretty much on its own, with no help from you or your new partner. You might not even notice it, but it'll start to follow you around.

From there, around the time your relationship starts to look like it has some kind of future, which is also around the time you look back and realize you've got a real history, you ease into the next phase. You become engaged, or you move in together, or you put it out there in whatever ways seem appropriate that you're in this thing for the long haul. You share a house, a name, a life, and you're stamped by this all-important relationship, in a great many ways. You're still an individual, but now you're also a part of something else, something bigger than just you . . . you're a recognizable brand.

You stay together long enough, you start cranking out all these kids, and they start cranking out all these kids, and over time you've got all these different generations coming out of this one relationship, and when that happens you're a full-fledged lifestyle. You've got your rituals and traditions. If you're one of those old-school, old-money families from England, you've even got your family shields and crests. You've got your own roles within your group, your special ways of interacting, and your special talents that you put out into the world. You're like the Waltons, the Jacksons, the Wayans . . . or, at least, your own, stripped-down version.

You look back and think, *Hey, look what we've managed to build.* And it all flows in a direct way from how you got together, how you stayed together, how you grew together. It flows from when you were just an "item," to how you've built your brand.

The Personal Hard-Sell

We sell ourselves at the office, so it makes sense that we sell ourselves everywhere else, right? Really, our everyday interactions with other people end up defining us every bit as much as our romantic relationships and our decisions and strategies at work. They signal what we're about, even when we don't mean to put out any signals. They allow us to sell ourselves, even when we don't appear to be selling anything.

They give us shape.

Think about it: how many times over the course of a typical day do you find yourself in a position to make a positive impression? Hundreds, probably. Maybe thousands. We create a constant, fluid, ever-changing impression, and we need to pay attention to that impression at every turn, or else our "brand" will get away from us. We'll think we're putting out one set of signals, while in reality we could be putting out a whole other message, and at the other end we'll get to wondering why other people don't see us the way we see ourselves. Here I don't worry too much about first impressions or lasting impressions or the impressions in between. It's the impression of the moment that counts. It's how you come across when you come across.

Yeah, first impressions are important. I get that. Every business book I read, talks about how you only get one chance to make a first impression. But it's become a cliché, so you won't read it here. Instead, you'll read that a first impression can be revised and improved upon. If it doesn't go the way you want, go at it again. Every time we make a move, we change the picture we put out to the rest of the world. We make a statement. It can be something as trivial as the beverage we keep on our desk at work. If it's a Diet Coke, it tells our colleagues we're careful about our weight, but not so concerned about artificial sweeteners. If it's a Big Gulp container from 7-Eleven, it says we don't care at all about our weight or our general nutritional intake—and not only that, we don't care who knows it. (Man, those suckers are big! Sixty-four ounces!) If it's a Snapple, it announces that we reach for the best stuff on earth, just as one of those designer, all-natural fruit drinks says we're concerned with what we put into our bodies. Red Bull? Well, that puts it out there that we're a hard charger, burning it at both ends, determined to keep sharp. And bottled water? Well, once again, we're back to our *item, label, brand, lifestyle* discussion. (Believe me, I can apply my theory to almost *anything*!) If it's a generic bottle of water, it sells us as simple, straightforward, no-frills, but if we've gone off the deep end and reached for that designer bottle of Bling H_2O it sets us up as just plain crazy.

We're all about the packaging, and this is especially true when you're talking about . . . well, packaging. Stay with me on this: I know that when I sort through a pile of mail in my office, my eyes will always be pulled towards that FedEx, UPS, or premium shipping envelope. That's why I talked about this in that list of calling-card strategies, because it's an easy and effective way to call attention to your material. There's something about those distinctive envelopes and mailers tells me there's an important message or document inside, worth the few extra dollars it cost to get it to me overnight. At least, that's the perception, and as we all know by now perception is half the deal. It tells me something about the person who sent it, too. That he or she is willing to spend a couple bucks to get noticed. And guess what? Almost all of those packages get right through to the CEO, or whoever it is in that corner office you're looking to impress, because it announces itself as important. Again, that's the perception. They stand out in the pile, and when I open up the package ahead of all the others, perception has to match up with reality.

They have to justify my interest, or I'm gone.

Rise and Shine

Our personal brand can change with each passing moment, and it's how we anticipate these moments and react to them that define us. Let's say you roll out of bed in the morning and stumble into the bathroom. Maybe you're in a little bit of a rush, because you hit that "snooze" button a time or two—transactions that begin to stamp your day without you really realizing it, because without meaning to you've put yourself in catch-up mode, hurrying to make up for a certain chunk of time you'll now think you've lost. It affects your mood, your outlook, so you start out a little hurried, or harried. Already, there's a negative shade to the way you see your day unfolding, but you don't even think about this. It just happens, and you just press on.

You go through the motions of getting started on your morning, same as every other day, before you head out to work. You check yourself in the mirror. You don't like all those lines and bags under your eyes. You don't like what's going on with your hair. You decide the outfit you'd laid out the night before doesn't really match your mood. So you do something about it. One by one, you address each little piece of uncertainty. You reach for some concealer to cover those lines. You put some styling gel in your hair to get control of that mess. You grab a different shirt from your closet to change up your look. You set in motion a whole sequence of events that all go to how you'll present or package yourself to the world in the next few hours. Or maybe you don't . . . but that's a part of the transaction, too. Maybe you decide to wear that *wrong* outfit, or go out with your hair a mess, or hide your eyes behind a pair of sunglasses.

With each move, each *transaction*, you consider your appearance. The kind of person you've become. The kind of person you'd *like* to be. The kind of signals you'd like to send, maybe even how you'll respond to the signals you receive. You're feeling brandish —there's that word again!—only here it's happening in a below-the-surface way. You're moving by pure instinct, when no one's watching and you're hardly paying attention, assessing the image you want to put across. Considering the effort that goes in to every tweak or adjustment. Accepting the kind of message you'll put out when you step beyond your front door and come into contact with someone else. Or maybe you won't even make it to that front door before your image starts to take its new shape. Maybe you're married, or in a relationship, and you'll emerge from that bathroom and have some type of exchange with your spouse or partner. *That* changes your picture. Maybe you're living with your parents, and you'll run into one of them in the hallway and they'll check you out and start in on how you're living, the choices you're making, what they think you should be doing with your life. *That* changes your picture, too. Maybe you've got a roommate, or a nosy neighbor, or a frisky poodle who needs your attention—and how you start off with each will change your picture as well.

It's like a row of dominoes, and the way each one falls has everything to do with the way the next one will fall.

And the one after that.

Creating an Impression

Break it down in just this way and you start to see how important it is—how essential!—to pay attention to each and every transaction or interaction, because each one goes into the mix of who we are and how we choose to come across. And don't ever forget the fact that we're *choosing* at every step along the way. It's an active, willful series of actions and inactions that, taken together, give us shape and character and presence. We make a first impression, and a second impression, and eventually a lasting impression, but let's never forget that we can *choose* to respond in a positive, hopeful way to an unexpected turn, or we can *choose* to make it a disappointment. We can *choose* to fix our hair or to leave it alone. At each impasse or moment of indecision, we're creating one of those impressions, but it's never a freeze-frame impression. It's not an over-and-out kind of deal or some still photo of what we want to look like or how we want people to see us, or a representation of our best self that we can send out into the world and hope it sticks. It's constantly changing, and it changes by the moment, so if we're smart and proactive about it we'll make sure that each *choice* we make about our presentation helps us to shine in the most favorable light.

We'll *choose* positivity. We'll *choose* to do the right thing. We'll choose to give it our best shot.

Again, this happens for some of us without a conscious thought. For others, it's all we can think about. Somewhere in between is where you want to be. Not so obsessed with your appearance or demeanor that you're gripped with constant worry over the tiniest, most insignificant detail, like what kind of drink you've got on your desk at work, and not so oblivious to the package of signals we put together each day that you miss out on any opportunities to show yourself to advantage. Something to keep in mind, but not necessarily in a front and center sort of way. Just file it away in the back, or off to the side.

Think of each day like a series of pitch meetings or job interviews. You want to get the gig, so you put your best foot forward. At every turn. Sometimes, things will go well. Other times . . . not so much. That's okay, but if you make a conscious effort to put a positive spin on each encounter, you'll wind up ahead of the curve. That spouse or partner, lying in bed next to you when your alarm goes off for the second or third time? A kiss on the check or a smile or a gentle pat on the rump will go a long way towards determining how you'll interact with each other for the rest of the day. Ignore your partner, or maybe twist up your face in disgust or disappointment at the mess of clothes he or she might have left at the foot of the bed, and you'll establish a negative tone that can't help but spill over into the rest of your day.

Maybe there's a kid or two underfoot, and they're tugging at you as you're trying to get ready for work, pleading with you to stay home with them. How you separate from them will mean everything to you as you set off on your commute and go on your appointments and everything to them as they get ready for school. It can go well or it can go not-so-well, but it will all flow in some way from this first encounter.

On the way to work you might hear one of your favorite songs on the radio, and that'll put you in a good mood. Or, you might be pulled over for speeding or running a stop sign, and as the cop walks over to your car you'll start to think how you might deflect or diffuse the situation. Surely, you'll think, there's a way to play this interaction to advantage, or at least to minimize the damage, so you'll scramble through every possible outcome. You'll come up with some line or hustle or strategy. Here again, a smile might do the trick—although I'd advise against a kiss on the cheek or a gentle pat on the butt. Chances are you'll take a quick glance in the rear-view mirror and see how those lines under your eyes are looking, and you'll weigh the odds of sweet talking your way out of a ticket.

Or, you'll stop for coffee, and the long line will either leave you despairing and frantic, or offer a refreshing point of pause before the day kicks in at full tilt. The girl behind the counter might get your order wrong, and you can get all indignant about it and leave the coffee shop feeling tense and agitated, or you can pleasantly point out the mistake and perhaps be surprised with a complimentary donut for your care and consideration. Or maybe there won't be a free donut in it for you, but you'll feel good about the exchange just the same and you'll leave that coffee shop with a spring in your step.

When you've got some time, start making a list of each and every one of these transactions you face in a typical day. Walk around with a notepad and write everything down. *Everything!* Before you know it, that list will stretch to pages and pages, because we're confronted with hundreds and hundreds of these moments every time we leave the house. And, hundreds and hundreds more every time we get home. The idea is to present your best self at each turn, to grab each opportunity to make a positive impression and find a way to attach it to your ever-changing personal brand. Yeah, you'll mess up a time or two. There might even be some days when you can't seem to get anything right. But the more of these interactions and transactions you can meet and complete to the good, the more your life and your prospects will improve along the way.

Like I said early on, it's a cumulative thing, so why not get started on your *'cumulatin'*?

Tweets and Pokes and Profiles
Naturally, it's no longer enough to limit these personal branding efforts to our face-to-face encounters. Now it's on us to spend the same time and energy on our virtual presentations, and a corresponding amount of time on the other side, trying to figure out what people are hoping to present.

The rise of social networking sites like MySpace, Facebook, and Twitter has set things up so that we feel the need to billboard our likes and dislikes and wants and needs for the world to see. I'm fascinated by these sites. Really, really. I'm on them all the time, building and extending my own brand, assessing and reassessing what other people put out about themselves or their goods and services, and what's remarkable about these sites is how easily they allow us to identify each other's brands, and how transparent some people can be with how they choose to be seen.

Bounce around with me on Facebook for a bit and you'll get what I mean. Here's a girl from Brooklyn, with 717 friends. Her status page tells us she's amazed by all of her birthday wishes and that she just got in from drinks at such and such club. She's bartending next week at some other club in town and hopes everyone will come down. Okay, so right away we get that this is a social, active person, maybe even a bit of a flirt. She's out there, circulating and determined to have a good time. Her profile picture is somewhat provocative, but then we start looking at some of the photos she's posted and we see that she's young, she's got a great body, and a great-looking group of friends. Everything appears to be right there on the surface: designer clothes, designer accessories, designer vacations. There seems to be a lot of drinking going on in these pictures, so our "friend" clearly likes to party, but then we open up her Information tab and see that she likes to watch a show called "Forensic Science," so she's clearly had some education—or, at least, she wants to present as much. She lists several different jobs, which tells me she has trouble focusing on any one thing or that she's still waiting for her first big opportunity. And here's a biggie: she posts that she's "engaged" but there are a couple hundred pictures of her photo page and she's not wearing a ring in a single one of them.

Hmmm . . .

In just a few seconds, I can scroll past the photos, postings and updates and get a good idea of this girl's "brand"—and she can change it at any time, with just a couple of keystrokes. And that's before I start checking out her network of friends, the points of connection that will reach out all across the city and paint a fuller picture of this girl's life, her hopes, her dreams. It's all *right there*, and corporate America is catching on to this phenomenon. In HR departments all around the world, the people who hire and fire are checking us out, because these sites offer the biggest, boldest, most thorough resumes out there. In certain segments of some Asian cultures, I'm told, people are even using these personal pages as a kind of status indicator, helping families decide who their sons and daughter might date or marry.

Not too long ago, I took a leap of Facebook faith and followed up with a girl from Los Angeles who was a persistent fan. She kept posting these messages, telling me how much she wanted to meet me, how much she wanted to work with me, how much I'd inspired her. On the surface, it was kind of cool, to be on the receiving end of those kind of props, but I didn't just jump to respond. I checked her out first. I saw on her Facebook page that she spoke four languages. I saw from her pictures that she seemed to hang out with classy, respectful people. Among her favorite books, she listed my last book, *Display of Power*, which I took to be not only a savvy bit of brown-nosing but also a great show of taste. She also listed a bunch of business titles that I'd read and admired. She listened to jazz, and mentioned Sade as a particular favorite. And, most impressive of all, she didn't have a pile up of Facebook friends—maybe 150 in all, which told me she was discriminating in who she hung out with. She wasn't just some random, flighty, frivolous person. She was thoughtful. She seemed to value her time and her friendships.

Really, I couldn't find a single red flag to scare me away from this person, so I sent her a return message on Facebook, telling her I was going to be in town and suggesting a place to meet. I thought maybe there might be a good fit, and that this person could actually make a contribution to our company and help extend our brand, but I never heard back. After a couple days, I had to skip town, and I thought that was that, but then a week or so later I got another message from this person, telling me that she doesn't check her Facebook all the time, and that she was so sorry she missed me. She hoped she hadn't missed her shot. I was back in New York by this point, so I told her to chill and that we'd find another time to get together. A couple weeks later, I was out in L.A. on some business, and we finally had a chance to meet face-to-face, and not too long after that the young woman is just a couple weeks into a six-month internship with our company, so you never know how these things turn out.

On Facebook, everybody's brand-ish, in one way or another. We package ourselves in the most appealing way we can, hoping to put it out to our friends and colleagues and causal acquaintances that our lives are going okay, that we're happy and healthy and productive. You don't find too many people selling themselves short. Instead, they go out of their way to put a positive spin on pretty much everything. You can even jump to the conclusion that when someone doesn't put up a profile picture it's because they're not too happy with their appearance—or, too lazy to figure out how to upload a photo.

On Twitter, it's basically the same. Different format, same story. You set it up so people know what you want them to know about you. You put it out there, whatever happens to be on your mind, only you don't do this in a scattered, off-the-cuff way. You spend some time on it. You count up those characters and work to get your thoughts down exactly right, and you know that other people are out there doing the same thing. Here again, if you pay attention to this type of stuff, you can read between the lines and figure someone out . . . maybe in a way they don't really intend. You'll look at a profile of some girl from Kansas. She'll write, "I'm a cool, chill person who loves life, despite what's being thrown at me lately. I live in Kinsley, but not for long." Right there, you'll know that she's having some trouble in one of her relationships. Whatever went down, it's got her thinking of picking up and moving, so this is clearly a girl in transition. Ready to make a change. Look a little further and you'll note that she's following 691 people, including Amy Winehouse, the English singer-songwriter who's famously in and out of rehab. A lot of times, you can tell what someone is going through on Twitter by the celebrities she follows, and here the link suggests that maybe this girl is struggling with some substance abuse issues of her own. Maybe that's what's behind her cryptic comment that she won't be in town for long. Or maybe there's nothing to the connection at all, but it's still something to think about—because, hey, most people don't announce their association or alliance with a troubled artist unless there's a real and powerful connection. You can also pay attention to how many followers that person has, and you can follow those threads and see where they take you. You can see whether or not she answers everyone who reaches out to her, how long she's been on Twitter, and all these other indicators, and at the other end you'll have a full portrait.

Sometimes it happens that you stumble across someone's work, and you respond to the fact that that person's work has been featured on a page belonging to someone you've chosen to follow. That happened with me and an artist named Paul Bush, who did a great portrait for me that I posted on my Twitter page. All of a sudden, he told me, he was getting all these hits from people wanting to find out more about his work, so it offers the kind of viral connection that feeds on itself. It gets bigger and bigger as our list of connections gets bigger and bigger.

Be careful, though. Whatever you post online is there for all to see. Might not make a lot of sense to tweet about your new job in a way you wouldn't want your new bosses to come across. Use some common sense. Don't go crowing about your big fat paycheck at your boring new job unless you're prepared for your comments to come back to bite you—because they most certainly will.

Read between the lines, fill in the blanks, connect the dots . . . do whatever you have to do, but the picture becomes clear soon enough.

The Cult of Personality

It was inevitable that this social networking phenomenon would slip into the corporate mainstream. A lot of companies have been slow to pick up on this, but some of our more visionary market leaders are out there, putting MySpace and Facebook and Twitter to work for them and their brands in a big-time way. Personally, I love how easy it is to set up a contest or some other interactive strategy to engage the thousands of people who've chosen to follow me on Twitter. I'll come up with some easy question for them to respond to, or some other way to engage them in a new product or personal appearance, and in this way help to build that all-important sense of belonging. Remember, your customers don't just want to buy your clothes or your fragrance or your beverage; they want to belong to a movement, a lifestyle, and a positive, ongoing interaction on a networking site like Twitter can help accomplish that.

Now, I want to be careful here, because these sites can change on you in an instant. As I write this, MySpace has been a force for five or six years, Facebook for three or four, and Twitter has been making noise for a year or so. And each network has changed its look and its focus many times along the way, so it's tough to talk about them with any kind of certainty going forward.

That said, I think it's a safe bet that some version of this type of viral, electronic networking will be with us for the next while, and the forward-looking business leaders and corporations will be out in front, riding the wave of all these changes. That's where I plan to be—and it's where you should be, too. Doesn't matter how high you've climbed on the corporate ladder. Doesn't matter how low you still happen to be. If you want to get to that next rung, you'll need to reach out in an electronic way to extend your brand—and, if you're out to push your brand to that next level, I can't think of a stronger, more cost-effective way than to marry the traditional marketing efforts you're used to paying for with some type of free social networking presence.

Media analysts have started grouping these networking sites into a bundle known as "social media," and in its current form it encourages users to weigh in with musings and anecdotes and insights about their lives and careers, in the hopes of connecting with others who might share a similar point of view. They sprung up to fill a perceived need on a social, interpersonal level, although lately we've started to see a whole mess of CEO-types (and, junior CEO-types) posting online. They've cast themselves as ambassadors for their different brands, and they're hoping to extend the reach of those brands in this exciting new way. They're reaching out to customers and helping them feel a part of their movement or lifestyle. In the process, they're creating a whole new space to promote their product or service, somewhere between the voice of the individual and the voice of the brand itself. At some companies, they've even got people on the full-time payroll coming up with 140-character Twitter observations throughout the day, which strikes me as a little extreme. There are some CEOs out there who manage their own thoughts just fine—like yours truly!

Executives at companies like Kodak, Best Buy, Cisco and Zappos.com are out there making noise on Twitter each and every day, with hundreds of thousands of followers. And they're at it all the time. They have to be. A stale or stagnant Twitter account is like an old billboard on the side of the road, advertising a movie that opened a couple years back. It's no longer relevant, of course, but even more troubling is how it sends the message that the people who posted it can't take the time or trouble to keep it current. That's way worse than not posting at all. You've got to feed that Twitter beast, a couple times a day, or you'll come across like some old coot trying to pass among us young'uns. Yeah, it can be a chore, but you need to nurture it and make it a part of your day, or else what's the point? Tell us what you had for lunch, if that feels like the message you want to put across, but also tell us what's next for your company. Tell us what you're thinking about regarding your next project, your competition, your new line. Help us get excited about whatever it is that's got you and your colleagues excited. Set it up so we're riding shotgun with you and your team as you go about your day.

Shaquille O'Neal caught some heat during the 2008-09 basketball season, for tweeting from the bench during an NBA game, and even though I can certainly see the controversy in having a professional athlete showing such a lack of focus during a game, I can also see the point. The social media contract is meant to put the people who follow you inside your head and inside your day-to-day. To let them feel like they're with you, part of the conversation. That's the intimate relationship you're after here, and if you're not up to it you'll be better off leaving this particular type of social media for some other executive at some other company. It doesn't get much more intimate than hearing from a player on the bench during a professional game, right? It's better than being a fly on the locker room wall. You're in the huddle, in the mix.

Shaq's not the only one, of course. Rappers step off the stage after a concert and fire off a "tweet" to their followers, letting them know how the show felt to them. Actors "tweet" backstage at the Oscars, right after they've grabbed one of those statues. Fortune 500-types "tweet" when the ink is barely dry on a merger or acquisition. Television news-people check in with an extra thought or two on a breaking story.

Do it right, play the game the way it's meant to be played, and your social networking efforts can be a real game changer for your company—or for the personal brand you're intertwining with your business. And don't feel like you've got to limit yourself to the tiny box of ideas available to you on Facebook or Twitter. Go out and start blogging, and find a way to drive your customers to your long-form insights through one of these sites. Say what you think needs saying, with no constraints. Run an interactive contest, through Facebook or Twitter, that invites your friends and follow-ers to your own website to participate. Your fans will either take the time to participate or they won't, but you'll get your point across.

Some things to keep in mind, as you plug into one of these social media sites:

- Be certain your observations are in line with your company's vision and agenda. If you're working at Philip Morris, say, and your company makes and markets cigarettes, it's probably not a good idea to vent virally about some idiot smoking at the table next to you in a downtown café.

- Give yourself a "tweet" target each week, and do your best to hit it. Make sure it's a manageable number—somewhere between 30-50 to start, which works out to about five or six each day. If it feels like a chore to keep up with your posts, you might want to think of some other strategy to promote your brand. You'll only succeed in this effort if it's not really an effort—meaning, you need to sign on in a sincere way. Your followers will see right through you if it looks like you're "phoning it in" or going through the motions.

- Keep it real. Don't go off on some ridiculous tangent that's got nothing at all to do with your product or service. Don't go making promises to your customers that you can't keep. And even if you need some help writing your "tweets" and posting them in a timely manner, don't ever appear less than genuine. It's okay to grab at an assist, and it's even okay to admit to having some help in this area, but you don't want your posts to come across as manufactured in any way.

- Cultivate your followers. It's not enough to start "tweeting" and be done with it. You've got to let folks know how to follow you, and jump on to other people's threads and invite them to join you on yours. You'll need to make an aggressive push, to start. After that, your followers will start coming to you. At some point, you'll reach the stage where you'll have 10,000 followers, or 20,000; 200,000 or 300,000; as your numbers grow, so does your reach. You'll look up and realize you've created an important asset for your company, a direct line to your customer base.

In every industry, in every segment, there are companies reaching out across this virtual landscape and tapping into a whole new market. At Whole Foods, just to offer up one example, there's a real back-and-forth going on between customers and management, an open discussion forum focusing on the Whole Foods lifestyle, complete with recipes, dieting, and exercise strategies and upcoming in-store promotions. That makes sense for them. As the CEO of FUBU, it makes sense for me to get and keep a dialogue going with our customers about the clothes they wear, the clubs they go to, and the music they like to listen to. On a personal level, these days I'm all about helping people realize their true potential, so I use my time on Twitter to offer motivational tips, or to highlight trends or developments that have something to teach us. If Twitter had been around when we were just getting going on FUBU, I might have approached my posts a little differently. I might have talked about our upcoming promotional events, or videos folks could catch on MTV or BET that featured our latest line.

But times have changed, and I'm doing what I can to keep up. Hit me up on Facebook (Daymond–John) or follow me on Twitter (@thesharkdaymond) and see what I mean.

Branded!

"The very first law in advertising is to avoid the concrete promise and cultivate the delightfully vague."

—Bill Cosby

NINE
Swimming with the Sharks

Back to my Mark Burnett story, with which I opened the book. When I left off, I was fully prepared to walk away from the prospect of working with Mark on the American version of his reality business show, which he was planning to call *Shark Tank* here in the US. It seemed like a sound, winning idea, primarily because of Mark's involvement and its successful history overseas, but sometimes you have to step away from a great opportunity. Sometimes you have to let a good one go in order to keep true to the values that got you where you were in the first place.

I hadn't even met with Mark personally on this, and once it appeared my involvement would get in the way of a commitment I'd made to my friend Khloe Kardashian, I figured that would just be the end of it. And it was, for a while. Until a couple of days later, when I got a follow-up call from one of Mark's producers. Apparently, my hard-to-get approach had made these guys want me on their show all the more, only I wasn't playing hard-to-get, and this wasn't any kind of approach. This was just me, keeping my word, sticking true to my brand, even if it seemed to cut against my best interests—or, at least, an opportunity to grow my career in an interesting new direction. I just thought this go-round with Mark Burnett wasn't meant to be, and hoped I'd get a shot at another at some point.

As it played out, though, "at some point" came around pretty quick. Without telling me what they were doing, the Burnett people hunted down the producer of *Keeping Up with the Kardashians*, to see what the deal was with my involvement on the show going forward. They found this poor woman in the middle of a ski vacation with her family, and to this day I don't know if they asked her to release me from my commitment or promised her an opportunity with Burnett's production company somewhere down the road, but at the other end of that phone call she was willing to give me up like a bad idea. She apparently said something like, "Ah, I don't think we'll be using Daymond at all, so I don't see what the hold up is. Tell Daymond he can do what he wants."

While I was on the phone with Mark's producer, filling me in on what went down on that call, my phone flashed with an incoming call from Khloe. I bounced off the Burnett call for a quick second, just to see what she wanted, and when I caught her up with what was going on, she said, "Are you out of your mind, D?"

I explained to Khloe that I was on the other line with Burnett's office, and that I would call her right back, but she was firm on this. She said, "Don't even think about calling me back or talking to me ever again if you don't make a deal with these guys and do this show."

I was dizzy by the time I bounced back to that call with the Burnett people. There were all these wheels spinning, separate and apart from anything I was doing on my end, and now it appeared the way had been cleared for me to sign on to this *Shark Tank* show—even though I hadn't really given all that much thought to whether or not it was right for me. It's like all these people were deciding what I should do next, based on whatever perception they had of who I was and what I stood for, and I didn't even have a vote or a voice.

Pretty amazing, don't you think? The way our personal brands can do a whole lot of business for us, even when we choose not to do business for ourselves? Anyway, now that this one contractual hurdle was cleared, I still had a bunch of questions—questions I hadn't pursued with any kind of due diligence because it seemed like the deal wasn't going to happen. Like I said, I still wasn't sure I wanted to get involved on *Shark Tank*, but the idea of working with Mark Burnett and his far-reaching brand was a powerful lure—so powerful, in fact, that I eventually threw up my hands and signed on. I figured either it would work out, or it wouldn't, but now that my conscience was cleared on the Khloe commitment, it was certainly worth a shot.

By this point, the producers had lined up the other "sharks" who'd be sitting in the tank with me, putting these entrepreneurs through their paces, and coming together to make a strong panel. Predictably, Mark Cuban was nowhere near this thing, but there were some interesting names on the list. There was New York City real-estate mogul Barbara Corcoran, infomercial pioneer Kevin Harrington, financial expert Kevin O'Leary and technology innovator Robert Herjavec. Some of them I'd heard of, some of them I hadn't, but they were all dynamic and forceful personalities. Add this reluctant fashion mogul to the mix, and you had a chill blend of backgrounds and sensibilities and areas of expertise.

The first time we got together as a group, I started to feel like we could really make some noise with this thing. There was a good fit all around, and as we got through our first couple of days of taping I recognized that we each had our own carefully cultivated personas. Our brands couldn't help but shine through the format of the show and our roles on Burnett's panel of experts.

Let's start with Kevin Harrington. I took to calling him "Sergeant," because he wears a crew cut for no apparent reason. As far as I know, he's never been in the military, but he carries himself like he has. He's so intense, so focused, and it comes across that he's deeply interested in whatever you put in front of him. Really, this guy analyzes everything, and his memory is just incredible. He made his money and his reputation as an infomercial producer, and he likes to think he can sell anything. That's basically his worldview: he tends to see the world in terms of what he can sell. We sit right next to each other on the *Shark Tank* panel, and the vibe that bounces off this guy is that he's very honest, very straightforward—a complete gentleman. My favorite thing about Kevin is that he carries around this big book, and he reaches for it to support whatever point he's trying to make. We might be looking at a new product, or talking about a new development in some industry or other, and it'll remind him of some project he worked on. It might have been last week, last year, or last century. He'll say something like, "Oh, I did an infomercial on that in 1972," and then he'll open his book of clippings and articles and fill in the details. Maybe it wasn't even his product, but he'll usually find a way to tie whatever we're considering on the show to some other business or innovation or marketing campaign. As such, I guess you could say his brand is that he's the ultimate salesman, with a great radar for the marketplace.

Barbara Corcoran comes across in private as the funniest person you're likely to meet. On television, and around a conference table, she's dead-on serious, but when she's not working she can crack you up. It's disarming, some of the stuff that comes out of this woman's mouth, and I suppose that's one of her great strengths as a businesswoman. She can cut through the ice and tension of any moment with a great line—and it's not always to set people at ease with a laugh, because sometimes she's just saying what needs saying. She's a real softie, though; she comes across on our set like a branding queen, because she buys into almost every idea that gets pitched to us. She seems to want to trust everybody and find the hope and possibility in every prospect. Sometimes, I watch her connect with one of the contestants on our show and I get to thinking Barbara is almost too sweet, the way she's quick to buy in to whatever these people are selling. It makes me see why she's so successful in real estate, where everyone is selling the same thing, because people want to do business with her. The same way she trusts in people, people trust in her. She's a people person, and her skill set is that she finds a way to let the buyer *and* the seller feel like they're special. Whoever she's dealing with, on whichever side of the deal, that's where she places her trust and her enthusiasm.

Robert Herjavec is another funny cat. He's Croatian, by way of Canada, and he made his money in the software business. And he made a lot of it, apparently. He also made a name for himself on the Canadian version of the show, *Dragon's Den*, so he's the only one with experience in this setting. He knows the drill. He's comfortable on set and in front of the camera. He actually comes across as mean and menacing on our show, but he's just the opposite off-camera. He's like a kid in a candy store, one of those people who really enjoys himself. Plus, he's a very shrewd businessman. I have enormous respect for the way he breaks down a potential deal and takes all the emotion out of it. The rest of us get sucked in to the personalities across from us, coming up with their creative pitches, but Robert cuts through all of that and gets to the core of a deal.

Then there's our other Kevin, Kevin O'Leary. I call him Mean

Kevin, because that's his persona on the show. It's like he did his own assessment of the field, recognized that all the other spots were taken, and decided to play the "bad cop" to our "good cops." He sits in the middle, and a lot of the hosting duties seem to fall to him, but he comes up with the best lines on the show. Unfortunately, some of those lines can be tough for some of our contestants to hear, because Mean Kevin gives it to them straight. He's a venture capitalist by trade, so he doesn't have it in him to be soft about money. He's all about the cash, he tells the truth, and he doesn't stop to think about hurt feelings, so there's no sugarcoating with this guy. But then the cameras go off and we're done for the day, and he morphs into a completely different guy. I don't know how Mister Rogers was when he left his "neighborhood." Maybe he was a complete jerk. But Kevin is just the opposite of how he comes across on the show. Away from the set, if you're not talking money, he's a sweetheart.

Me, I fit myself into the pop culture slot on the panel. Fashion, music, lifestyle goods and services . . . those are my stock in trade, and whenever we have to consider a deal in one of these areas, the other sharks tend to look to me for guidance. My thing is to root like crazy for the little guy, because it wasn't that long ago at FUBU that we were little guys ourselves. We started out small, so I have tremendous respect for these mom 'n pop types who come to our set looking for an assist. A lot of times, you can have the best idea on the planet but you don't have the resources to put that idea into play, so I try to keep that in mind when we consider some of these deals— because, hey, you never know when you might come across the next big thing.

◆◆◆

For those of you who haven't seen the show, it's set up like *American Idol* or *Dancing with the Stars* or pretty much every other show where the contestant has to pitch or audition in front of a panel of judges or experts. The twist here is that people are pitching business ideas—new products, sideline opportunities, upstart ventures. During our first round of tapings, we heard hundreds of pitches, and I had no real idea where or how our producers find these good people. And yet somehow they keep coming up with all these hardworking, innovative entrepreneurs, desperate for an infusion of capital or expertise to help them take their ideas to the next level. After we hear their pitch, which can range from the silly to the serious to the sublime, it's up to each of us sharks to decide if we want to invest our time or our money in the idea going forward. We can do this individually, or as a group. Usually, the person will come in with a hoped-for deal—say, $250,000 for 25 percent of his or her business. Do the math, and that means the person values his or her business at $1 million—but then we sharks do our own math and come up with our own valuation. We might like a product or a concept, but based on current sales we might put a different price tag on the company—maybe $500,000. That means we might invest $250,000, but only for half the company in return.

Everything's negotiable, including whether or not we'll do a deal at all, and that's where the show gets its sizzle. Some of the ideas we turn down flat, and others only seem to interest one or two of us; occasionally, we'll meet with someone who impresses the entire panel, and when that happens the sharks might start negotiating against each other for their best deals. Or, we'll pair off and throw in together, in groups of two or three. Remember, the way the show is set up is that we're spending our own money on these projects, so we're pretty careful with our interest. It's one thing to throw Mark Burnett's money at some of the hair-brained ideas we hear on the show, but it's another thing to put our own money at risk, so we tread lightly.

Right away, I started to see there were basically two kinds of pitches. There's the person who comes in with an idea or a product he or she is really passionate about, and lights up the room in such a way that we want to do business with them. When that happens, the power of the brand is in the strength and the vision and the personality of the individual making the pitch. As investors, we're willing to make a mistake on a deal like this, because we're betting on the individual. Usually, that's a safe bet. We're putting our money in the good hands of someone who believes in what they're doing or making or selling. For example, a woman came to us with a product she called "The Turbo Baster"—a three-in-one type kitchen utensil that was a baster, a brush, and another few things besides, all designed to help you cook a roast or a turkey in a more efficient way. It was actually an ingenious design, and it left a few of us scratching our heads and wondering, *Hey, why didn't I think of that?* There was a basic prototype, but the woman behind it hadn't really figured out how to mass produce it. She didn't know how much to charge for it, how to take it to market . . . anything. And, as I recall, she had no real business plan, so there wasn't much to it other than the woman herself, and that's where the product stood out. Really, this woman was so lovable, so energetic, so enthusiastic about her product and its potential that Kevin ended up investing in it, just on the strength of this woman's personality.

After another pitch, Barbara invested in a playful little elephant medicine dropper, created to help parents dispense medicine to their children, and the product was clever and well-designed but the real appeal was the woman who came up with it. She'd battled cancer and was taking care of an autistic kid at home, and she was such an inspiring, appealing presence on our set that Barbara couldn't help but buy in.

The other pitches we buy into are patents. Somebody will come to us with a new product or invention that no one else can touch. It's unique, it's protected, and it's strong enough that we start to think we can make some money with it. What we found, though, pretty early on, was that we still had to have some sort of feel for the person making the pitch, because if we didn't want to be in business with that person there was no design in the world that could interest us. Here's what I mean: this guy came to us with a great idea for an enhanced seat-belt item that would protect the driver or passenger automatically. The only problem was, this guy had been really devastated by an accident, which had been the inspiration behind his innovation. He had his heart set on personally installing the item in an after-market way, in a local body shop, which of course greatly diminished the potential. Robert wanted the patent, with an eye towards selling it to one of the big car manufacturers, who would be in a position to mass produce it and install it directly in their new line of cars. But Robert wanted no part of the inventor, who seemed intent on letting his emotions run his company, so ultimately Robert backed away from a deal. Robert's approach would have net sales in the millions, while the inventor was apparently content to sell in the hundreds, and this the kind of stuff you have to figure out when you're going into a partnership. The discussion might start with an idea or a business or a product, but in the end it will come down to personality.

Similarly, we heard from an imaginative guitar manufacturer who was making and marketing a kind of "air" guitar—a completely workable, playable guitar that could be bent and folded in such a way that it could be packed pretty easily. Man, it was a pretty ingenious design; you could fold the neck, almost in half, and the instrument would stay in tune. But instead of being willing to license the design to a big guitar company like Gibson or Fender, this guy wanted to handle the production himself, so none of the sharks were interested. Our thinking was, *Hey, you've got to take your emotion out of the deal and recognize that business is business.*

After hearing pitch after pitch after pitch and hot idea after hot idea, I caught myself paying more attention to the personalities than to the real and tangible opportunities these good people were trying to present. Yeah, innovation is key. Building a better mousetrap is key. And, like my mother always said, thinking big is key. But the real key, even on a reality television show, is how you come across; success in business comes down to how you carry yourself and the image you present—to your customers, to your competitors, and to your potential partners and investors. If you've got an up-and-running business, and you're making some money, investors will still steer clear if they don't like you as a person, or they don't feel like they can trust you or that you'll work hard for them. On the other side, if you've got no business plan and just a vague idea, they might throw in with you just because they admire your enthusiasm or your work ethic.

And so the great lesson of my time on *Shark Tank* is this: our personal brand matters most of all, and we need to pay attention to it, nurture it, and make sure it fits with whatever we're doing or making or selling. Real and tangible business happens in the balance between the personal and the professional. It's basic. How do you want people to describe you? That's the takeaway, in every exchange, all the way down to our central relationships. Do you want your wife to say, "Aw, I've got to go home to see my *damn* husband?" Or, "Yay, I get to go home to see my husband?" It might seem like a small difference, and if we're being completely honest we'll have to admit that from time to time both sentiments might apply, but the difference is everything. And, *recognizing* the difference is everything . . . and more.

Here it is, in bite-size, Tweet-appropriate form: understand how other people see you and you're in a better position to see yourself.

That said, I'm not advising readers to please people to death. That's no way to be, either. Be true to who you are. Stay in tune with yourself and what's important to you. Don't go kissing other people's butts just to get what you want. But make sure that the vibe you put out into the world is the vibe the world is taking in. Don't be surprised by the way other people see you. If you're determined to be an unpleasant, difficult person, then be the *most* unpleasant, *most* difficult person you can be, but know that's how you're coming across. If you mean to be pleasant and easy going, though, and you're still coming across as a giant pain, then you've got some soul searching to do—as well as some re-branding.

Look in the mirror and see what comes back, and take it from there. Let's face it, appearances don't lie. They can be deceiving, but the best sales job in the world can't get past your true self—the brand within.

FB

COOGI

WWW.DAYMONDJOHN.COM

CROWNHOLDER

OPULENCE

DISPLAY OF POWER
FOUNDATION

www.displayofpower.com

Want to put the power of "The Brand Within" to work in your life?

Build the brand within YOU guided by Daymond himself at:
www.displayofpower.com.

Use the promotion code **BRAND001** to get a 90 day trial membership and become a member of the **Display of Power Community.**

Be a part of:

1. Live video discussions with Daymond John himself.

2. Background materials on each chapter.

3. Podcasts of the book.

4. Guides to building your personal brand in business and life.

5. Interviews with Daymond John and special guests.

6. An interactive discussion forum.

7. And new EXCLUSIVE CONTENT added regularly.

Daymond walks like he talks and the principles he lives by have helped him build a global mega-brand from nothing. Learn how to unleash your inner mogul with Daymond at your side.

The first step is NOW, go to www.displayofpower.com

Unleash the Brand Within
RISE TO POWER
www.displayofpower.com